SHATTERED,
BUT NOT
BROKEN

SHATTERED,
BUT NOT
BROKEN

(Only Because of His Grace)

KATHY ANN TAYLOR

XULON PRESS

Xulon Press
2301 Lucien Way #415
Maitland, FL 32751
407.339.4217
www.xulonpress.com

Printed in the United States of America.

ISBN-13: 978-1-6628-1382-5

TABLE OF CONTENTS

ACKNOWLEDGMENTS

FIRST, I WOULD LIKE TO THANK MY LORD and Savior, Jesus Christ, for giving me this opportunity to share with you the words in this book. If it were not for Him, for the unction of the Holy Spirit, these words would never have been penned to paper.

Second, I thank my husband of thirty-three-plus years for supporting me throughout this endeavor—for his encouragement every step of the way and for his love and support, even when he didn't know he was doing so.

Third, I am thankful to our children for allowing their lives to be put on display so that others may know that God's grace and mercy prevail throughout the good times and the not-so-good times. And, most importantly, His mercy never runs out!

I certainly want to thank my siblings, Tommy, Brenda, Annie Marie, Alisha, Beverly, and Paul, for their encouragement and love over the years, for putting up with me throughout the not-so-good years, and for extending their prayers, support, and patience and not giving up on me when I was a "wretch undone."

I am also eternally grateful to the following:

My church, Family of Grace, with Pastors George Lee and Karen Glass, and everyone who is a part of this congregation, for standing in the gap with me during the time of my husband's illness and throughout this present time. I am grateful for their provision of meals, transportation, and, most of all, their prayers, worship, and praise.

A big thank you to my dear sisters-in law, Diane Johnson, Shirley Rigmaiden, and Rita Harris, for their unending encouragements. When I needed a shoulder to cry on, they were right there.

To my forever friends and sisters in Christ, Reneé Abshire, Veronica Ashworth, and Elizabeth Ann Standridge, who untiringly answered my texts when I needed an explanation to a dream, called me with the confirmation to a dream I had, and, when I was at the end of my rope, provided whatever I needed to have the strength to hold on just a little bit longer.

Certainly, I thank my friends Cliff and Jeanette Hill and their son, Jaye, for their answer to my Macedonian call the night my husband fell ill. Without their quick response, I don't know how that event would have turned out. I am forever grateful.

There were other churches in the community that were lifting us up to the throne room of God during that trying time. Among them were Starlight Baptist Church, Star of Bethlehem, St. Mary's COGIC, God's Temple of Refuge, Norris Memorial COGIC, and Mt. Canaan. Please forgive me if I have omitted any names; charge it to my mind and not my heart. For everything that was done for us, I am forever grateful, and I pray that God will richly and openly reward you for your compassionate giving of yourselves to me and my family.

INTRODUCTION

The Spirit of the Lord God is upon me; because
the Lord hath anointed me to preach good tidings
unto the meek; He hath sent me to bind up the
brokenhearted, to proclaim liberty of the captives,
and the opening of the prison to them that are
bound; to proclaim the acceptable year of the Lord,
and the day of vengeance of our God; to comfort
all that mourn; to appoint unto them that mourn in
Zion, to give unto them beauty for ashes, the oil
of joy for mourning, the garment of praise for the
spirit of heaviness; that they might be called trees
of righteousness, the planting of the Lord, that He
might be glorified.
Isaiah 61:1–3

I HAVE KNOWN FOR A LONG TIME THAT
I was called to write. Even before I was given this ministry
call as indicated by this scripture in Isaiah, I knew that
God had been birthing in me a word to the nations. I am
not sure of the exact year when it happened, but God
gave me a word that I was being "called out." I didn't
understand what that meant at the time and thought I was
being called to the streets for evangelism. Even though

that may be a part of what He was saying, as I wrote this book, I understood more clearly that He was actually saying that the words I would pen to page would be my "calling out." This book will reach people all over the world, wherever the Lord might send it.

I am reminded of the scripture in Psalm 45:1: "My heart is inditing a good matter: I speak of the things which I have made touching the king: my tongue is the pen of a ready writer." I write the words of this book with great excitement, knowing that this is the will of God, knowing that those who read these words will be touched by the Spirit of the Lord God who gave me every word to say. I prayed that the Spirit of God would guide and inspire me, and each time I sat down to write, the words would begin to flow. Toward the end of the year, I felt an urgency in my spirit to complete the writing. It was as if the Lord was saying, "Okay, Kathy, get going, get it finished. It is time for it to go out to the world." And so I would begin afresh, because there was a cause.

A cause is a reason or motive for some action. There is a reason why you and I must stand firm in the face of opposition. Do you think the enemy wanted this book to go out? Of course not! There were many days when I was distracted from writing. Some days, I would not go into my study at all, putting off the writing for another day. But then I would hear some of the words that I had already written in the book in a sermon that day, or someone would call me on the phone and start talking about the very things that I had written in the book. This was God's way of confirming to me that yes, He did indeed intend for me to write this book, no matter what the enemy was saying to the contrary.

The cause, or reason, for this book is for a husband and wife to live in a fulfilled marriage where the union is exactly as God purposed it to be—for the husband to love his wife as Christ loves the church, for the woman to honor, cherish, and respect her husband in the same manner, and for the two to become one.

The cause is to see your sons and daughters become the men and women they were destined to be before the world began—to see them walk in the divine purposes of God Himself, to live a life fully pleasing to the Father, and ultimately to bring glory to His name and His kingdom.

The cause is to see the plan and purposes of God come to pass in your life and in your ministry, even though you may be going through turbulence, dealing with deceitful people, and enduring mistreatment. No matter what may be going on in your life, you have to be determined and stay determined to have all that God said you could have. The devil will tell you to quit and stop believing because it is not worth it. But the devil is a liar, and all he wants to do is to stop you from coming into the greatness that the Father has promised to you as a believer. The adverse things we see happening in our families' lives are only temporary. At some point, we have to say to the enemy, "Devil, enough is enough!" You see, it is God's name that is at stake—not yours and certainly not mine.

There is a cause because our God will keep that which has been committed to Him against that day.

To see the cause come to pass, there is a battle raging that is beyond human strength. Jude describes it as "[saving] some by snatching them from the very flames of hell itself" (Jude 23).

So I stand in the midst of turmoil, dreams that may not yet have come to pass, and the light afflictions that accompany this life and announce to all the demons in hell, "You will not have my life, my husband's life, our children's lives, or our families' lives, because Jesus disarmed you and made a public example of you, triumphing over you" (Col. 2:15).

I stand with and for all of you believing that the one in whom we have put our trust will do everything that He has said He will do—no matter what.

Just keep trusting!
Keep believing!
Keep standing firm on His promises!

SHATTERED, BUT NOT BROKEN
(Only Because of His Grace)

As I began to write this book, I was reminded of a song that I fell in love with after listening to it a million times. The name of this song is "God's Grace" by Rev. Luther Barnes. I want to share some of the words of this song because it fits so beautifully with my story:
How did I make it all these years?
How did I make it this far?
Through the valleys and over the hills,
I know it had to be God.
How did I make it through the storm?
How did I make it through the rain?
If you want to know, just how I got here, it's so easy to explain.
It was God's grace (God's grace)
I made it this far (I made it this far)
By the grace of God.

I remember the times when I strayed away,
Even though I knew the Word,
Still I wouldn't obey,
But God's mercy and His grace stayed with me and
brought me,
Brought me all the way.
Some people said, (God's grace)
They said I wouldn't make it (God's grace)
Some people said (God's grace)
I wouldn't be here today (God's grace)
But look at me, look at me I made it this far
By the grace of God.
And I thank You (God's grace)
Thank You Jesus, (God's grace)
Lord I thank You, (God's grace)
Thank You right now, Jesus (God's grace)
I made it, (I made it this far)
I made it (by the grace of God).

I certainly did not deserve either His mercy or His grace, but in spite of myself, He lavishly extended both to me. For that I will be eternally grateful.

As I give you the words I put on the pages of this book, I pray that you will come away with the knowledge that none of this has anything to do with me. It is all about Him, my Lord and Savior, Jesus Christ—the one who brought me through it all. Even though I went through the fire, I came out without a hint of smoke on me, no traces that I had even been in a fire. The Word of God is certainly true, as it says in Isaiah 43:2, "When thou passest through the waters, I will be with thee; and through the rivers, they shall not overflow thee: when thou walkest through the fire, thou shalt not be burned; neither shall the flame kindle upon thee." I could have perished—but God!

IN THE BEGINNING

MY LIFE DIDN'T BEGIN WITH TRAGEDY. I was the third oldest of eight children, the oldest of five daughters born to our mother, Annie Mae O'Banion. Today, there are seven living siblings, our oldest brother, Ellis Eugene Rigmaiden, having died many years back from lupus complications.

Our mother was the daughter of Fannie M. Wright, our grandmother. Mama Fannie, as we lovingly called her, was a beautiful soul. She had the most loving spirit, and she could make us laugh and cry all at the same time. We knew that our grandmother loved us, even if she did run us out of the house whenever her "stories" came on television. She would do all of her work early, and when the time for her stories came, she shooed us outside to play. We dared not bother her until all the stories were over.

Our grandmother came from a loving family, of which she was the next to the youngest. Her father was Thomas H. Powell, and her mother was Fannie Powell. At the time that I came along, my mother was single, and because I was a girl and the older siblings at that time were boys,

I was allowed to go and live with my great-aunt and great-uncle Lloyd and Rosa Self, who lived in Leesville, Louisiana. My great-aunt could not have children, so she asked Mother if she could raise me, to which my mother agreed.

I didn't realize at the time that this was God's plan for my life. This was where it all began. God knew that the enemy of my soul was trying even then to snuff out my life, and God was saving me alive. Later in life, my great-aunt told me that as a little girl, I would have episodes where I would literally lose consciousness and my great-uncle would have to take me to the hospital. She didn't give me the reason for these episodes, so I surmised this was a ploy of the devil to end my life before I could do damage to his kingdom.

Living with my great-aunt and great-uncle, I was raised as an only child, even though I had sisters and brothers. I would visit my siblings during holidays and summer vacations. My great-aunt was not working at the time, so she had the time to teach me how to read and write. When I began attending school at six years old, I was already reading at a sixth-grade level. My great-aunt nurtured a love for reading within me, and books became my best friends.

I so enjoyed reading, You could always tell where I had been in the house because there would be a book lying about. During the summer, I enjoyed visiting the library and would come away with five or six books at a time, and within two weeks, I had finished reading them all. My great-uncle did his part in cultivating my love for books, too. During the summer, he required me to study the Constitution and to memorize the preamble before I could go outside to play. Little did I know just how important this love for books was, and how it would play a major role in my life.

When I was ten, my great-uncle told me one day that I would be going to a different school. At the time, I was attending Vernon High School, which included all grades in one school. But in a short space of time, he informed me, I would be transferring to Leesville Elementary School. As a child, I didn't understand that I was going to be a part of history—the integration of schools. My great-uncle had volunteered me to be one of three black students to make the transition to formerly all-white schools.

All the work that my great-aunt and great-uncle had instilled in me, prompting me to read, to study hard, to discipline myself to do homework first before going outside to play, did not go without reward. I was able to go to Leesville Elementary and hold my head high because I maintained an A average in the midst of this confusing time of transition and upheaval. It was difficult, to say the least, having come from a school where everyone looked the same and going to a school where I was the one who looked different. However, my great-aunt had always taught me to hold my head up, to know that I was just as important as anyone else and that no one was any better than I was. She taught me to look a person straight in the eyes when speaking and to stand up for myself, especially if I knew what I was saying was right. As a result of her efforts, I was able to go into that school and carry those convictions with me. I was not intimidated by anyone because I knew who I was. I was somebody! Namely, a child of God!

This brings to my mind the Scripture verse in Jeremiah 29:11: "For I know the thoughts that I think toward you [Kathy], saith the Lord, thoughts of peace, and not of evil, to give you an expected end." God placed me in this situation because He knew what He had placed within me. He afforded me an opportunity to walk alongside those who did not understand that the color of my skin did not make me different from them. Thankfully, He had used my great-aunt and great-uncle to instill in me values, high self-esteem, and a secure identity.

However, later in life, when I was walking with my eyes wide shut, I would stray from knowing who I was. But thank God for Jesus, who will not allow us to continue on that wrong path. He brought me back to the remembrance of who I was and to whom I belonged. But that story comes further on in the book.

I remember, as a child, always attending church, even though my great-aunt and great-uncle did not. I would walk across the road to a little Methodist church, where I first began to learn about God. I didn't really understand much, but I knew Someone was always there.

Interestingly, in this church, there was no talk about Jesus, just God. As a result, later in my life, perhaps in my early twenties, when I heard someone talking about Jesus, I was surprised and confused. Hearing about the Savior, I questioned in my mind, Who is this Jesus, and what part does He play with God? As if that was not enough, you can imagine my surprise when I heard about the Holy Ghost. I was truly amazed. I could not fathom that there were actually three entities in the Godhead, when all I had ever heard about in my church was one. Nonetheless, I enjoyed attending church and hearing the teachings about the Lord.

I was baptized for the first time at ten years old in the Methodist church I attended. I was not immersed in water, but received a sprinkling of water on top of my head, along with others who had accepted Christ into their lives. We all stood in front of the church in a row, and the minister came down the line and sprinkled each one of us individually.

I remember my Aunt Sadie (my great-uncle's sister) taking me to church, where she played the piano and taught me how to sing. After I learned how to sing, she took me to different churches, where I would stand beside the piano as she played and sing hymns from the hymnbook. This gave me a love for singing, though I didn't understand then that I was worshiping God in song.

In retrospect, I can see that all these events were adding up to where I would be later in life. God had His hand on my life and would not let go, even though I was going to endure some hardships for a period of time. This worship that I was engaging in as a child, singing hymns to the Lord, was preparing the stage for the battles that would be waged against me by the enemy of my soul—but God would be right there.

At the age of seventeen, thinking that I was all grown-up, I met and married my first husband. Actually, my mother had to sign for me to marry because I was underage. This was the second time she allowed me to go away, the first time being when I was two years old and went to live with my great-aunt and great-uncle. I am reminded of an old saying that says, "When you really love something, you let it go." I know that my leaving at seventeen was hard for her, but she allowed me to make the choice to marry at such a young age. Little did I know that this would be only the beginning of many poor choices that I would make in life. But God was still there.

You see, many years before this—in fact, I was eight years old at the time—I had repented of my sins and asked God to forgive me. I had told my great-aunt a lie, and she found out about it. She was disappointed in me, which I overheard her telling her best friend on the phone. So that night, I got on my knees and asked God to forgive me for telling her that lie. I truly had godly sorrow over it. Then I went to her and asked her to forgive me. Though that did not stop me from making many wrong choices later in life, it did lay a foundation. Even though I didn't understand much about repentance the night I repented of my sin, it was the beginning of understanding that I could turn to the Lord and He would not turn me away.

Just like my mother allowed me to make choices that were not good for me, God did the same. He knew what was best, but I was determined to do things my way. Both my mother and the Lord loved me enough to allow me to go down a dark and slippery path. My mother didn't know if I would make it out of that miry pit, but she never stopped praying for me. However, God knew that I would one day come to myself, as the prodigal son did, and turn back to the Father who loves me. But it would be a long journey before that would happen.

THE JOURNEY:
From a Mess to a Blessing

GOD USES EVERYTHING FOR OUR GOOD. Sometimes God uses the most painful journeys in our lives to prepare us for authority and bigger responsibility. You could never have told me that the things I suffered in my early twenties were preparing me for where I would be later in life. It was so hard during that time that sometimes I despaired even of life. I wondered where God was, not realizing He was there all the time.

When I say that God uses everything for our good, it reminds me of the Word of God in Matthew 14:14–20 (emphasis added):

And Jesus went forth, and saw a great multitude, and was moved with compassion toward them, and He healed their sick. And when it was evening, His disciples came to Him, saying, This is a desert place, and the time is now past; send the multitude away, that they may go into the villages, and buy themselves victuals. But Jesus said unto them, They need not depart; give ye them to eat. And they say unto Him, We have here but five loaves, and two fishes. He said, Bring them hither to me. And He commanded the multitude to sit down on the grass, and took the five loaves and the two fishes, and looking up to heaven, He blessed, and brake, and gave the loaves to His disciples, and the disciples to the multitude. And they did all eat, and were filled; and they took up of the fragments that remained twelve baskets full.

The fragments were the leftovers; to some, they would not have been important enough to keep and would have been thrown away. But Jesus knew that the fragments, the leftovers, were just as important as the meal itself.

My pain, hurt, disappointments, and emotional and physical abuse were detrimental, to say the least, but God used the items left over from that time to bring healing and restoration to my life and the lives of others. You see, we are not to waste our pain, but use it to heal others. I know that sounds strange; it did to me during those turbulent times. How in the world was someone else going to be healed by the pain I was suffering? This was what I wondered in my finite mind. However, God knew that later in my life, I would work at a women's shelter and share my journey with other women who were going through the same thing. He also knew that other women who needed to hear that they could come out of the abuse they were struggling in would come across my path. Who better to let them know that they could make it but someone who had gone through it and come out of it alive? Only by the grace of God was that possible.

Everything in life is either God-ordained or God-allowed. God did not send this pain into my life; it was God-allowed. The life that I was living was the result of my own decisions, prompted by the thoughts put into my mind by the enemy. At the time, I actually thought they were my thoughts. The Word says it this way in James 1:13–15: "Let no man say when he is tempted, I am tempted of God. For God cannot be tempted with evil, neither tempteth He any man: But every man is tempted, when he is drawn away of his own lust, and enticed. Then when lust hath conceived, it bringeth forth sin: and sin, when it is finished, bringeth forth death."

The enemy only plants the seed in our minds to do things that are totally contrary to God's Word and will for us. It is not sin until we act upon these thoughts. The enemy has only three tactics to use against us, and he uses them over and over: (1) the lust of the flesh, (2) the lust of the eyes, and (3) the pride of life. As the head of this world's system, he amplifies our attraction to the world. He knows exactly who and what to bring into our lives to derail us from the course God has set for us.

This is exactly what happened in my life. I accepted what the enemy offered, and from that moment on, I embarked on a roller-coaster ride with the devil himself. It was a time of utter confusion and devastation. I walked with my head down, though I had always carried myself with an air of confidence before, because this is what my great-aunt had taught me. But when this travesty happened in my life, I lost all sense of self-worth, and I began to feel as if this is what I deserved.

I imagine this is how Adam felt in the garden after the fall. As Genesis 3:6–7 tells us, "And when the woman saw that the tree was good for food, and that it was pleasant to the eyes, and a tree to be desired to make one wise, she took of the fruit thereof, and did eat, and gave also unto her husband with her, and he did eat. And the eyes of them both were opened, and they knew that they were naked, and they sewed fig leaves together, and made themselves aprons." Both Adam and Eve realized they had done something that was not right. Similarly, I knew my life had taken a wrong turn because of my choices, but I didn't know how to get back to where I needed to be.

As I said before, God was right there in the midst of it all. He even gave me a dream one day as I lay across my bed. I dreamed that I was driving a vehicle down the road, and a huge black bull was headed directly for me. There was no way to get out of the bull's path. To make it worse, I had my children and others in the car with me. As I tried to turn the car around to keep from hitting the bull head-on, I looked in the backseat and saw that my friend had grabbed my baby and stepped out of the vehicle. I screamed and awakened! This dream unnerved me, but I couldn't figure out what it meant. Later on that night, however, I was to find out, and in a most shocking fashion.

I was driving back home, and there were others in the car with me. I realized that I had missed my turn, so I began turning around in the road. To my utter horror, I had not seen an eighteen-wheeler that was coming, and it was right in front of me. Just at that moment, in the middle of the road, my car stalled. There was nowhere to go. Remembering the dream, I looked back to see if my child was still in the vehicle, and he was, but my friend had gone out the door. Somehow, I got the vehicle cranked, but I do not know how in the world that truck did not run completely over us. I know now that it was God protecting us from what would have been a fatal accident. At the exact moment when that truck was barreling down upon us, He must have dispatched His angels to keep the truck from running right over the top of us.

The bull in my dream represented the eighteen-wheeler. God was warning me that something was about to happen.

He was letting me know that I needed to turn around, to change the course of my life before it was too late. The bull in my dream was huge and black and represented all the evil the enemy could muster. He wanted to take me out, to steal my life before I could turn back to the Lord who loves me. But God!

I would like to say that this was the point where I finally turned things around and walked away from the life I was living, but sadly, that was not the case. I continued in disobedience against God. Because this is what it was—disobedience. According to The New Strong's Complete Dictionary, the word disobedient is marah, meaning "to rebel or resist; to provoke." I was resistant to everything I had been taught in the Word. I was living according to my flesh and was blinded by the enemy.

The Word tells us in 2 Timothy 1:7, "For God hath not given us the spirit of fear; but of power, and of love, and of a sound mind." Certainly, the fear I was experiencing in my life was not from God, but from the devil himself. He had placed a stronghold upon me so fierce that I could not in my own strength break free of it. But thank God for Jesus and a praying mother and grandmother who did not give up on me. I had a family that knew the power of prayer. This is how I escaped from the grip of the enemy. There is a song I learned in the Church of God in Christ that says, "Devil thought he had me, I got away." Yes, thank God for Jesus, I got away!

One thing I would like to share, which I feel is of utmost importance, is if you find yourself in a situation like this, do not allow the enemy to isolate you from your family. The enemy knows that if he can get you by yourself, he can have a field day with you. If he can get your loved ones to turn their backs on you and give up on you, he can have his way more easily. When you are isolated, the enemy can interject his thoughts into your mind and make you believe they are your own thoughts.

Sometimes the enemy will try to convince you that the pain you are experiencing is a part of you, that the suffering is your identity. This can lead you to accept a victim mentality, and this is exactly where I was. I had a victim mentality. I did not remember that Jesus had died for me so that I didn't have to live within the prison of pain and rejection the enemy had trapped me in. I just needed to stop clinging to what was broken (my life and my way of thinking) and embrace the new wineskin Jesus offered.

None of us can fix the past, but all of us can create a much better world for ourselves and our families. Paul says it this way in Philippians 3:13–14, "Brethren, I count not myself to have apprehended: but this one thing I do, forgetting those things which are behind, and reaching forth unto those things which are before, I press toward the mark for the prize of the high calling of God in Christ Jesus" (emphasis added).

I continued to merely exist. I was not truly living, but simply going through the motions. Each day I went to work, but even that was a haphazard event. I could not fully put myself into my job because I was living in a war zone at home. I didn't know what was going to happen from one day to the next. It was a nightmare, but I was wide awake. I tried to make it through each day, but it soon became too much to handle. I had held this job with the welfare office for nine years, but in the ninth year, I was fired because I couldn't get to work on time, and even when I was there, I could not focus on the tasks at hand.

12

I remember a story from T. D. Jakes in his book He Motions. In it he told a story about a man who loved exotic fish and had a large fifty-gallon aquarium in his apartment. Because the man traveled, he equipped the aquarium with a state-of-the-art mechanism that would automatically clean the tank, release food, and maintain a constant water temperature. One time after being out of town for several days, he returned home to find his beloved fish dead. The water had overheated and killed all the fish. He agonized over how the fish must have felt as the water grew hotter and hotter. He wondered if they had screamed in silence, wondering where he was and why he was not there to save them. Had they begged for someone, anyone, to turn down the temperature? As the owner shared this story with T. D. Jakes, his eyes began to tear up. The owner understood what it meant to emit a silent soul scream that no one can hear as the water around you increases from tepid, to warm, to boiling-point hot.

This is where I was. I was screaming in silence, wondering why no one heard me, wondering why no one would get me out of this mess or come to my rescue. It never registered that no one could hear me. After all, it was a silent scream, so who could hear that? Only one Person could—God. But God was the one I was running from, the one whom I was in disobedience to. I felt that surely He would not want to help me now. Why would He? All these years, seven to be exact, I had lived the way I wanted to live, did what I wanted to do. The enemy told me, through the mouth of the person with whom I had been living those seven years, "No one will come to your rescue. No one wants you anyway. You are ugly. You can't do anything right. What a mess!" After a consistent diet of these kinds of words, I began to believe them to be true.

I had forgotten what the Word of God says in Psalm 139:

> Whither shall I go from thy spirit? Or whither shall I
> flee from thy presence? If I ascend up into heaven,
> thou art there: if I make my bed in hell, behold,
> Thou art there. If I take the wings of the morning,
> and dwell in the uttermost parts of the sea; even
> there shall Thy hand lead me, and Thy right hand
> shall hold me. If I say, Surely the darkness shall
> cover me; even the night shall be light about me.
> Yea, the darkness hideth not from Thee; but the
> night shineth as the day; the darkness and the light
> are both alike to Thee. For Thou hast possessed
> my reins; Thou hast covered me in my mother's
> womb. I will praise Thee; for I am fearfully and
> wonderfully made: marvelous are Thy works; and
> that my soul knoweth right well.

God loved me! If no one else did, not even myself, He did.
However, in that weary state of mind, I could not fathom
how the Creator of the universe could love a wretch like
me. What I didn't realize was the truth of verses 15–18
in Psalm 139:

My substance was not hid from Thee when I was made
in secret, and curiously wrought in the lowest parts of
the earth. Thine eyes did see my substance, yet being
unperfect; and in Thy book all my members were written,
which in continuance were fashioned, when as yet there
was none of them. How precious also are Thy thoughts
unto me, O God! How great is the sum of them! If I should
count them, they are more in number than the sand: when
I awake, I am still with Thee.

I was so numb from the constant battle of trying to survive
from day to day that I could in no way understand how

precious I was in His eyes. I couldn't comprehend that He thought about me all the time. There was not a day that went by that He didn't think about me. He knew my dilemma, my heartache, my pain, but He is a gentleman and will not force Himself on any of us. We have to willingly open our hearts to Him. The Bible tells us that in Revelation 3:20: "Behold, I stand at the door, and knock: if any man hear My voice, and open the door, I will come in to him, and will sup with him, and he with Me."

This is an open invitation from Jesus. It does not expire; it has no time limit on it. Jesus is standing at the door of everyone's heart, and all that is required for Him to enter is for that person to open his heart. What stopped me from opening my heart? Fear, rejection, ridicule, inferiority complex, just to name a few. All those spirits had attached themselves to me and were weighing me down. As I said before, I walked with my head down in shame, not even believing that Jesus could love me. This is how the enemy kept me locked in the jail cell of my mind. I was walking around physically free, but in my mind, I was in lockdown and could not break free.

But you know, God always has a plan, and He had a plan for me to break through and to get out. God sent my cousin Maudie to me. I don't even remember how she found me, but one day I saw her, and we talked. She could tell something was not right, even though I did my best to hide it. She gave me her phone number and told me to call her if I needed to talk. She was working for a domestic abuse hotline that had just begun to operate in our city. I didn't even have a telephone at that time and would have to go across the street to use my neighbor's phone. (This was before the cell phone era.)

I didn't call her until some weeks later, however. I awakened that morning with the feeling, This is the day. This is the day when I will be free. This is the day when I will walk away from all this turmoil, despondency, and bondage and into a new day of freedom. Nevertheless, I began that day like any other. The two older boys caught the school bus, and I got the youngest child ready for the day. I had already packed his diaper bag with important papers that I would need, such as birth certificates, school records, vaccination records, and anything else I thought might be necessary. I had hidden this bag in the closet, hoping it would not be found.

So, that morning, after cleaning up the house and putting meat into the sink to thaw for supper, I walked out of that little house on Prickett Street to go call my cousin. She told me to go back to my house and wait for her there. True to her word, she soon arrived. I walked out of that house and did not look back, because I knew I was not ever going to return. I didn't want to take even one glance back and be reminded of the horrors I had endured in that house.

Because there was no shelter for women and their children in my location, we were taken to a shelter in Lake Charles in Calcasieu Parish. We didn't stay there long, however, because my middle son needed medical attention for a large boil that developed on the heel of his foot. I had no job at that time, so I returned to my mother's home. My sister then scheduled an appointment with the doctor for my son. His foot was soon lanced and the infection drained.

Next, I began the long road to recovery and restoration for me and my children. The search for employment was hard because not many jobs were available in the small town where I was living. Furthermore, I did not own a vehicle, so I had to make cold calls from out of the phone book. Our neighbor across the street, Mr. Robinson, God rest his soul, worked as a janitor at the First Baptist Church and asked if I wanted to work in place of one of the workers who was soon to undergo surgery. I eagerly accepted. I had never been a proud person who thought I was above working as a janitor, especially since I was the sole provider of my three sons. I worked there for three months, and then I was again back at square one, looking for a job.

One day I went to pay a bill at a rental store. I had been thinking that I would either go into the military or go live with my older brother and his family, who were living in Alexandria, Louisiana, at that time. As I was paying the bill, I made a remark about possibly leaving the area. The manager said, "Wait one minute." He then went into the back room, and when he came out, he said, "Would you like to work here? I went into the back to call the owner, and he told me to offer you the job." I eagerly accepted and began work the very next day. God was at work again, showing me that He was still there, that He had not left me.

One day I was talking with one of the customers, and she told me about an apartment on North Street. She advised me that the rent was based upon income and gave me the apartment manager's number to call. I did call and was told there was a two-bedroom apartment available. I didn't know anything about the "projects," but that was where the apartment was located. All I knew was that I would have a place for me and my children to live.

It wasn't that I was not grateful to stay with my mother and siblings, but I knew that as a woman, I needed my own place, and the children needed their own space, too. I was very appreciative to my mother for allowing us to stay with her but knew I needed to move on. So we did. My mother helped with some of the furniture, and I purchased a couch, television, coffee table, and dinette set with earnings from my job. I was so proud of my small apartment. It was not much, but it was clean, and it was mine.

When I returned to my mother's home after leaving the shelter in Lake Charles, I rededicated myself to the Lord. I was tired of the empty, unfulfilled life I had lived during those seven years that I was subjected to the tirades of the devil. So when I went to church that Sunday, my mind was made up to return to the Lord. After Sunday school, I talked with Rev. C. B. Norris, the pastor, during that time, and told him I wanted to return to my home church. He said to come back that night for the church service, which I did.

I knew it was going to be special because all the church mothers were there. You see, in the Church of God in Christ, the mothers of the church would tarry with you until you received the Holy Ghost. I imagine that Elder Norris figured that since I had been out in the world and away from the church for so long, I needed a lot of tarrying. But I didn't care, and I was not offended. I wanted to return to the Lord, and I didn't care what I had to do to get back to Him.

There is a song we used to sing titled "Take Me Back." It goes like this:

I feel that I'm so far from You, Lord.
But still I hear You calling me.
Those simple things that I once knew.
The memories are calling me.

I must confess, Lord, I've been blessed.
But yet my soul's not satisfied.
Renew my strength.
Restore my joy.
And dry my weeping eyes.
Oh Lord (take me back),
Oh Lord (take me back, dear Lord),
To the place,
Where I first received You.
Oh Lord (take me back),
I'm begging You to take me back.
(Take me back, dear Lord) To where I first believed.

This is where I was at this point in my life, and as I knelt at that altar with all those church mothers praying over me, I repented of all the wrong I had done during those years of disobedience. I was enveloped in the arms of my loving heavenly Father and washed clean, and my sins were forever thrown into the sea of forgetfulness, never to be remembered again. When I left there that night, I was filled with so much peace. I knew everything was going to be all right. And it was for a time, but then the enemy of my soul brought the same person back into my life.

IN THE FIGHT OF MY LIFE

YOU MIGHT ASK HOW IN THE WORLD I
allowed this to happen again. I asked myself that question a thousand times over, but no answer came, at least not at that time. Now, however, I understand the answer as found in the Word of God in Romans 7:14–25:

> For we know that the law is spiritual: but I am carnal, sold under sin. For that which I do I allow not: for what I would, that do I not, but what I hate, that do I. If then I do that which I would not, I consent unto the law that it is good. Now then it is no more I that do it, but sin that dwelleth in me. For I know that in me (that is, in my flesh,) dwelleth no good thing: for to will is present with me; but how to perform that which is good I find not. For the good that I would I do not: but the evil which I would not, that I do. Now if I do that I would not, it is no more I that do it, but sin that dwelleth in me. I find then a law, that, when I would do good, evil is present with me. For I delight in the law of God after the inward man: But I see another law in my members, warring against the law of my mind, and bringing me into captivity to the law of sin which is in my

members. O wretched man that I am! Who shall deliver me from the body of this death? I thank God through Jesus Christ our Lord. So then with the mind I myself serve the law of God; but with the flesh the law of sin.

Apart from the righteousness of Jesus Christ, we have absolutely no moral or spiritual goodness. We cannot trust in our own instincts or our own courage, as this will most assuredly fail us. Only as we acknowledge our weakness will we find the strength in Jesus Christ to withstand the enemy. Our only hope is to throw ourselves upon Jesus, who is the source of our strength. His grace is sufficient, and His strength is made perfect in our weakness (2 Cor. 12:9).

This is where I made my mistake: I felt I could handle the situation. I felt I was strong enough to take care of myself. However, I was not as strong as I thought. You see, the enemy knows our weaknesses, even though we try to cover them up. Yes, I was in church, I read the Bible, and I studied the Word, but still there was that seed of iniquity on the inside. There was a war raging on the inside of me.

The enemy was using all his strategies to try to defeat me. First Timothy 6:12 says to "fight the good fight of faith." In all my years of living, I had never been involved in a physical fight. Not wanting to confront anyone or cause anyone pain, I had never engaged in physical confrontations. Consequently, I didn't realize the true implication of Paul's words to Timothy. Actually, it was not a physical battle at all that I was facing, but a fight in the spiritual realm against a real demon, the enemy of my soul, and he doesn't play fair. In his kind of fighting, there are no rules. He doesn't wait for the bell to ring to come out and fight; he comes out before the bell, and if you are not ready and focused, he will beat you down.

The enemy has a strategy, and he uses it to the hilt. He doesn't care that you are in church; in fact, he wants to draw you out of your church, out of the protection of the covering over your life, out of the comfort of the sanctuary, and away from those with whom you worship. This was his ploy with me: to get me back to where I was in the past. You see, the devil is determined to use our yesterdays to keep us from spiritual advancement today. He never gives up reminding us of past mistakes, past hurts, past disappointments.

Just as he never gives up, we must never stop running the race set before us, according to Hebrews 12:1–2: "Wherefore seeing we also are compassed about with so great a cloud of witnesses, let us lay aside every weight, and the sin which doth so easily beset us, and let us run with patience the race that is set before us, looking unto Jesus the author and finisher of our faith; who for the joy that was set before Him endured the cross, despising the shame, and is set down at the right hand of the throne of God."

We can avoid looking behind us by keeping our eyes on Jesus, the champion who initiates and perfects our faith. I took my eyes off Jesus for a moment, thereby opening a door for the enemy to walk through, and I was not strong enough to close that door in my own strength. Thankfully, I had enough faith in God to know that He did have the strength to bring me out of this situation once again. I knew that He loved me, in spite of my weakness. As it says in Psalm 55:16, "As for me, I will call upon God; and the Lord shall save me." I was not going to go through seven more years—not even one more year—of torment again. I realized that I needed to get out of this situation. If the enemy had tracked me down again, I knew that this time he meant business and was not going to stop until he had destroyed me either physically or mentally. By this time, my children were older and beginning to see the things that were happening to their mother. But thanks be to God, who always causes us to triumph in Christ Jesus! He brought His plan about, once again, through my cousin.

At that time, my cousin lived in an area called Twin Lakes, which was not too far from my apartment. One day after work, I gathered up my boys, and we went to her home. I didn't stay, however, because I feared that somehow the person I was entangled with would find me there. I was afraid again. I did let the boys spend the night with my cousin, while I went to stay with a friend. The next day, I picked up my children and went back to live with my mother. My sisters cleaned out my apartment for me because I was afraid to even go back there. This was a roller-coaster ride that I was determined to get off and stay off.

A WONDERFUL CHANGE

I CONTINUED TO WORK AT THE RENTAL store. Years passed, and one day a tall, well-built young man walked into the store. I had seen him once or twice around town but had never spoken to him, nor he to me. As he turned in the tapes he had rented, I noticed his eyes sparkled as I waited on him. He remarked that he was enamored at how confident I was in my job. Little did he know how far along I had come in building up my confidence, because for a long time, I was anything but confident. I didn't have a lot to say to him that day, but I did give him my name when he asked. Before leaving, he handed me a slip of paper with his name and phone number and asked me to call him.

Because I had gone through so much turmoil in my life, I was very cautious, to say the least, so I didn't readily call his number. When he returned to turn in the tapes he had rented, he asked me why I hadn't called him. I simply said that I had been busy and hadn't had the time to call. He left the store again, and I still did not call. When he came into the store for the third time, he asked, "Is there something wrong with me?" I replied there was nothing wrong with him; I just had not called. That night, when I

25

got off work, I said to myself that I would call him, and I did. It was a really good conversation.

The next day, he called me at work, "just to hear my voice," he said. I smiled at the idea of him thinking about me enough to call just to hear my voice. So began a whirlwind of a courtship with this very romantic young man. It was so refreshing to be courted and made to feel like a special lady. He took me to Galveston, where he proposed. We have been married now for thirty-three years. Actually, we have been together for thirty-six years, because we lived together for three years before marriage. This is not something I am proud of, but I thank God that we both had a mind not to continue in sin, but to marry.

Marriage is not only a commitment, but also a covenant. We both took our marriage vows willingly, knowing that only death could bring them to an end. When I stood before my family and God that twenty-third day of January in 1988, I spoke these solemn words: "I, Kathy Ann Self Lynch, take thee, Larry J. Taylor, to be my lawfully wedded husband, to have and to hold from this day forward. For richer, for poorer, in sickness and in health, till death do us part. To love, honor, cherish, and obey. Forsaking all others, and thereto I plight thee my troth. In the name of the Father, the Son, and the Holy Ghost." I meant every word of what I was saying.

In my Bible, the Open Bible King James Version, is the explanation of how the first family began:

> Genesis 2:18–25 fills in the details of the simple statement in Genesis 1:27: "male and female created he them." This account particularly amplifies the "and female" part of the statement and shows how woman was created. Three

observations can be made on the passage that will help us to understand how the family began:

The need for woman (vv. 18–20). Woman is absolutely essential in God's plan. It was God who observed, "It is not good that the man should be alone" (v. 18), and determined to make a "help meet" for Adam. Woman's role in the will of God was to be a "help" who was suitable for Adam. Woman's role in the will of God was to be a "help" who was suitable to man in every particular mental, spiritual, emotional, social, and physical need. God undertook an orientation program to show man the need that He alone had observed. He brought to man the birds and beasts He had created, so that man should exercise his dominion over them (v. 28) and name them (v. 19). However, in verse 20 it is noted that for Adam there was no "help" similar to himself.

The provision of woman for man (vv. 21–24). God caused Adam to go to sleep, and God removed one of his "ribs." Exactly what God removed is not known, but it was adequate for His purpose. He "made" (lit., built) a woman (v. 22) whom Adam recognized as being his equal, "bone of my bones, and flesh of my flesh." This resulted in what has become known as the universal law of marriage (v. 24), in which it can be seen that: (1) the responsibility for marriage is on the man's shoulders—he is to "leave his father and mother," (2) the responsibility for keeping the union together is on the man's shoulders—he is to "cleave unto" (i.e., stick to) his wife, and (3) the union is indissoluble—"they shall be one flesh."

We continued in holy matrimony, raising my three sons together. We each had three children from our prior marriages, and his children visited at various times. We did our best to instill within them the concept to love each other because we were a family, albeit a blended family. They seemed to accept that idea, and to this day, these six children show love and concern for each other. It was not easy, this thing called marriage. We knew that we had to work at it if we were going to make it, and that is what we did.

The boys were always involved in some type of sports, which kept my husband and me busy bringing them to practice and games. We both loved it, though. I had played sports growing up, so it was exciting to see the guys excelling in athletics. Larry had also excelled in sports and took the time to teach them the fundamentals of football and basketball. He had never played baseball, but that didn't stop him from becoming a coach in order to keep up with them in this game. It was a busy time, but one that I would not take back for anything.

At the beginning of our marriage, my husband worked at the local paper mill, and I was still at the rental store. Then I decided to pursue a different career path, so I began to attend real estate classes at night after work. With the completion of ninety hours of real estate education with the Wingate School of Real Estate, I took the test and became a licensed Realtor. So began my return to the things I loved: God, education, and books.

After obtaining my Realtor license, I gained employment at June N. Jenkins Women's Shelter. I worked at Greg Cagle's real estate business during the morning hours and at noon went to work at the shelter. This continued for about five years, and then I left the real estate business but continued working at the shelter. I realized that not only was I helping others to understand the dynamics of the abuse they had suffered at the hands of their partner, but it was helping me as well. Little did I know, but I needed the release this work would eventually give me.

As I was talking with the director one day, she asked me about the abuse that I had suffered. I began to tell her, and as I did, tears began to flow. She told me this was an indication that I had not been completely healed of those hard things in my past. I didn't realize it, but up until that time, I had simply stuffed those experiences away, so when I opened up to tell her about them, the floodgates opened.

The Word of God says, "They that sow in tears shall reap in joy." The tears I had sown would one day lead me to victory over the past hurts and pain in my life. In my work at the shelter, I was able to help other women become victorious too. I let them know that I made it out of that situation only by the grace of God. I always emphasized that it was not me, but God who brought me out. I gave Him the glory that He so richly deserved, because it belonged to Him anyway.

I continued to work at the shelter and to grow stronger with each passing day. I was not only forgetting the things of the past, but I was also growing stronger each day in the Lord. One night I had a dream and in the dream I was at the church, Zion Hill, and appeared to be getting married, though at the time, I was already married to my husband. I was at the back of the church, preparing to walk down the aisle, when I noticed I was wearing a red dress. However, as I continued down the aisle, the dress got lighter and lighter, and by the time I reached the front of the church where the preacher was standing, my dress had turned completely white. This was the Lord's way of letting me know that I was going through a process of restoration. Even though I had started out with scarlet sins,

He was making them as white as snow. It was not going to happen overnight, but it would be a process. As Isaiah 1:11 says, "Come now, and let us reason together, saith the Lord: though your sins be as scarlet, they shall be as white as snow; though they be red like crimson, they shall be as wool."

God was calling me unto Himself, letting me know that I didn't have to be afraid to come to Him even though I had done so many things that were against His will. He was still saying, "Come, we can talk about these things. There is nothing you have done that I am not willing to forgive. Don't turn away, but continue to walk toward Me, because with every step you take, I will cleanse you of your unrighteousness." This is why the dress turned white with each step I took rather than all at once. With every step forward, it was "becoming" white.

I want you to know, reader, that God is ready, willing, and able to forgive. This is what it says in 1 John 1:9: "If we confess our sins, He is faithful and just to forgive us our sins, and to cleanse us from all unrighteousness." We confess the things we have done that were wrong, agreeing with Him that these things were wrong, and we express sorrow for doing them. He knows already that we did wrong, but He wants us to tell Him.

The word confess, in the Greek, means "to acknowledge or agree fully." We fully agree, we take total responsibility for our wrongs, we don't make excuses for them, and we don't say that someone else made us do them. This agreement or confession is spoken out of our mouths. Paul says it this way in 2 Corinthians 4:13: "But since we have the same spirit of faith, according to what is written, 'I believed and therefore I spoke,' we also believe and therefore speak." Faith that is in the spirit and heart of man must speak.

As the old song says, "It's me, O Lord, standing in the need of prayer. Not my mother, not my father, but it's me, O Lord." King David made this confession in Psalm 51 when the prophet Nathan confronted him about the wrong he had committed by having Uriah the Hittite killed in order to cover up his own sin with Bathsheba. After Nathan told him a story, David acknowledged his sin. He confessed, agreeing with the Lord that he was the man in the story. He freely admitted his sin, and then he asked God for forgiveness. God did forgive him, but the sword was never to depart from David's house.

The entire prophecy of the sword, with its surrounding context, is found in 2 Samuel 12:1–14:

> And the Lord sent Nathan unto David, and he came unto him, and said unto him, There were two men in one city; the one rich, and the other poor. The rich man had exceeding many flocks and herds: But the poor man had nothing, save one little ewe lamb, which he had bought and nourished up; and it grew up together with him, and with his children; it did eat of his own meat, and drank of his own cup and lay in his bosom, and was unto him as a daughter. And there came a traveller unto the rich man, and he spared to take of his own flock and of his own herd, to dress for the wayfaring man that was come unto him; but took the poor man's lamb, and dressed it for the man that was come to him. And David's anger was greatly kindled against the man; and he said to Nathan, As the Lord liveth, the man that hath done this thing shall surely die: And he shall restore the lamb fourfold,

because he did this thing, and because he had no pity. And Nathan said to David, Thou art the man. Thus saith the Lord God of Israel, I anointed thee king over Israel, and I delivered thee out of the hand of Saul; and I gave thee thy master's house, and thy master's wives into thy bosom, and gave thee the house of Israel and of Judah; and if that had been too little, I would moreover have given unto thee such and such things. Wherefore hast thou despised the commandment of the Lord, to do evil in His sight? Thou hast killed Uriah the Hittite with the sword, and hast taken his wife to be thy wife, and hast slain him with the sword of the children of Ammon. Now therefore, the sword shall never depart from thine house; because thou hast despised me, and hast taken the wife of Uriah the Hittite to be thy wife. Thus, saith the Lord, Behold, I will raise up evil against thee out of thine own house, and I will take thy wives before thine eyes, and give them unto thy neighbour, and he shall lie with thy wives in the sight of this sun. For thou didst it secretly; but I will do this thing before all Israel, and before the sun. And David said unto Nathan, I have sinned against the Lord. And Nathan said unto David, The Lord also hath put away thy sin; thou shalt not die. Howbeit, because by this deed thou hast given great occasion to the enemies of the Lord to blaspheme, the child also that is born unto thee shall surely die.

Make no mistake about it—whatever God says, He will do. Even though David was forgiven, the word that God spoke about the son born to David and Bathsheba came to pass. The baby died, even though David fasted and prayed, because God had spoken.

A TIME OF
RENEWAL AND GRACE

DURING THE EARLY YEARS OF OUR MAR-
riage, my husband and I went through a period of time
when we tried to have a baby. I went to an OB-GYN clinic
in Lake Charles because I thought I was expecting. The
doctor (who no longer practices) examined me and con-
curred that because of the enlargement of my womb, I
was indeed pregnant. I returned home and told Larry, and
he was so excited. Shortly afterward, I went to have the
lab work done, but it did not show a positive result for
pregnancy. The doctor said not to worry because it might
be too early for the results to show pregnancy. I therefore
went about my daily tasks and my job. A little later, I had
another appointment for lab work, and it again showed a
negative result. By this time, I was becoming a little nervous about the turn of events. Both times the doctor had
examined me in his office and said I appeared to be pregnant. Then I went to have the lab work done for a third
time, and again it showed a negative result.

At this point, I called my sister-in-law, Shirley, my older
brother's wife. They were still living in Alexandria at the

time. I asked her about the doctor she was seeing, as it occurred to me that I needed a second opinion. She gave me her doctor's name and office number; in the meantime, she also spoke with him when she went for her next appointment.

I was able to get an appointment with this doctor, and upon his examination, he scheduled a Pap smear, along with more lab work. When the results of the Pap smear came in, I received a call from the doctor's office. The nurse advised me that the Pap smear showed an abnormal reading. They therefore scheduled me to return to the doctor's office, where a biopsy was done. With the return of the biopsy, the doctor determined that I needed a complete hysterectomy and scheduled it immediately.

After the surgery, the doctor explained why my womb was swollen and giving the appearance of pregnancy when in fact I was not. He said that when they removed the cervix, they found cancer cells. I knew that it was God who had kept the cervix from spilling out any of the cancerous cells into other organs in my body. However, as a precaution, the doctor advised forty-five days of radiation.

Tears began to roll down my cheeks at this news. It was such a shock to hear the "C word." I began to think about my family, my husband, and my children, who were still in school at that time. I didn't want to leave them. All these thoughts flowed through my mind. My husband had returned home to take care of the children, and then he had gone to work. Thankfully, my mother and my older brother were there when the doctor gave me the news. I was in shock, but they both consoled me. Eventually, I got myself together, reminding myself that God is a healer, and no matter what, I had to stand on His Word.

I didn't have time to be sad about the situation because I was released the following Monday and was to begin the radiation treatments the following week. It was tough, to say the least, because my body had not completely healed from the surgery. Nevertheless, I had to undergo five days of inner radiation, which was to be followed by forty-five days of outer radiation.

On the first day of treatment, perhaps it would not have been so difficult if I had not had to wait so long for the hospital staff to attend to me. There were quite a few patients who were there to see the same doctor who was to give me the treatments. I had to be worked in, since I was not his regular patient, so I had to wait for an opening in his schedule for that day. As a result, I lay on a table for hours before anyone came to take me to the treatment room. I was in tears by the time my turn arrived, and as the treatment was on an outpatient basis, I still had to travel back to DeRidder by car, which was approximately an hour-and-a-half drive.

Needless to say, I decided not to go back the following day. The next day after that, I received a call from the doctor who had performed my surgery. The doctor who was overseeing the radiation treatments had called to let him know that I had not kept my appointment. I explained to the doctor how I had lain on that hospital cot for hours before anyone came to get me, and how much pain I endured that day. I told him emphatically that I was not going back again.

I am sure my doctor heard the note of finality in my voice and realized he had to say something to get my attention and relay to me the seriousness of not returning for the completion of the treatments. He talked to me as if I were part of his family, saying, "Mrs. Taylor, I am speaking to you as if you were my wife, and I love my wife dearly. You really need to undergo all these treatments. We need to make sure there was no spillage from the cervix when we removed it. This is the reason I am asking you to take the recommended days of radiation. It is a necessary precaution." He also spoke with Larry and explained the seriousness of it to him. I then agreed to return to the clinic the following day and also agreed to complete the entire forty-five days of treatment. I kept my word and returned the following day.

However, the same day I talked with my doctor about my treatment, I also talked with the Lord about it. I told God I really did not want to return to that clinic because I had endured so much pain that first day. As I was talking to the Lord, He reminded me of a book by Kenneth Hagin, Sr. titled The Triumphant Church. I pulled this book off the bookshelf in our study and began to read. The book talked about praising your way to victory. I knew that something supernatural had to happen if I were to be able to endure the remaining treatments.

I learned through reading this book that praising God is a form of spiritual warfare. Psalm 149:6 says, "Let the high praises of God be in their mouth, and a two-edged sword in their hand." It was not about how I felt, because I didn't feel like praising. I was nervous about what was to take place the next day, because thoughts of what had already taken place were floating around in my head. But I was determined to take God at His Word and do what He had said to do—praise.

This proved to be a turning point in my life. It made me aware of the fact that God will do exactly what He says He will do. I went into the clinic the next day with praise in my heart. As they were preparing me for the treatment,

I began to praise. I wasn't singing out loud, but in my heart, words of praise were ringing out loud and clear to the Lord.

Ephesians 5:19 says, "Speaking to yourselves in psalms and hymns and spiritual songs, singing and making melody in your heart to the Lord." Remember, I said earlier that my auntie had taught me how to sing, and I had sung in front of the congregations of many churches on many occasions. Well, these were the hymns that I was now pouring out to the Lord, song after song. Not only that, but all the songs I had sung in the choir at the church I attended as an adult were also there in my mind and in my heart.

Before I knew it, they were finished with the treatment for that day. Hallelujah! The Lord had brought me through it with no pain. The sacrifice of praise had stopped the enemy dead in his tracks; he didn't know what to do. I am sure he couldn't understand how the day before I was in tears, and on this day, I was smiling as I left the clinic. But I knew! Each day of my treatment, I came in with praise and left with praise. It became a vital part of my life.

God used this time of stillness in my life for me to get to know Him, to build a relationship with my Lord and Savior. Once you develop an intimate relationship with God, you will never be the same. On the days when my husband had to work and the boys were at school, I would go to the dining room table and open my Bible and begin to talk with the Lord. One day—I remember this so clearly—I told the Lord, "Lord, I hear people say that You talk to them, but You don't talk to me." Just as clearly as if someone were standing in the room, I heard a still, small voice say, Kathy, I do talk to you. I speak to you through My Word. Oh, the joy I felt to hear my Father say He speaks to me through His Word! He was letting me know that the way to hear His voice was to delve into His Word because His Word is who He is, and Jesus is the Word. What a marvelous feeling, what a sweet feeling, as I basked in His presence!

One day as my husband was taking me to the hospital in Alexandria for a treatment, I was feeling a little despondent. I guess you could say I was having a pity party, thinking about how long I had been out of work and how my husband had to take off work to drive me back and forth for the treatments. (When my husband could not take me, my brother and sister would do it.) The Lord, however, would not allow this feeling of despondency to continue.

As I was looking out the car window, He showed me the beautiful yellow flowers growing on the side of the road, and this scripture came to my mind, prompted by the Holy Spirit: "Consider the lilies how they grow: they toil not, they spin not; and yet I say unto you, that Solomon in all his glory was not arrayed like one of these. If then God so clothes the grass, which is today in the field, and tomorrow is cast into the oven; how much more will He clothe you, O ye of little faith?" (Luke 12:27–28). As I said previously, the Lord talks to me through His Word. He reminded me that if He could take care of something as small as the lilies of the field and the grass, He could certainly take care of me, His daughter. He had to bring back to me the remembrance of who I was and to whom I belonged.

Faith is the number one thing that the enemy fights us so hard on. He does not want our faith to grow, but grow it must. This growth process is described in the Word of God in 2 Peter 1:3–8:

According as His divine power hath given unto us all things that pertain unto life and godliness, through the knowledge of Him that hath called us to glory and virtue: Whereby are given unto us exceeding great and precious promises; that by these ye might be partakers of the divine nature, having escaped the corruption that is in the world through lust. And beside this, giving all diligence, add to your faith virtue; and to virtue knowledge; and to knowledge temperance; and to temperance patience; and to patience godliness; and to godliness brotherly kindness; and to brotherly kindness charity. For if these things be in you, and abound, they make you that ye shall neither be barren nor unfruitful in the knowledge of our Lord Jesus Christ.

This was a time of renewal and grace, my thoughts coming in line with His Word and His will for my life. I no longer had time to pity myself. In the passage quoted above, it says that He has given us all things that pertain unto life and godliness. According to Webster's dictionary, the word pertain means "to have to do with." So, we could say that His divine power has given us all things that have to do with life and godliness. He didn't just save me and fill me with His Spirit; He didn't just deliver me from the hand of the enemy who was trying to destroy me; He didn't just heal my body for me to sit down and think, Okay, I have it made now. I can just sit back and bask in the knowledge of knowing that He is a great God. No! He did all that so that I could grow in the knowledge of Him; and as I grew, all these things—faith, virtue, knowledge, temperance, patience, godliness, brotherly kindness, and charity— would abound in me so that I would become fruitful.

This is what Jesus said in John 15:16: "Ye have not chosen Me, but I have chosen you, and ordained [appointed] you, that ye should go and bring forth fruit, and that your fruit should remain [abide]: that whatsoever ye shall ask of the Father in my name, He may give it you." I came to understand that He was the one who chose me; I didn't actually choose Him. If we are truthful about our situations, we all would have to 'fess up and say, "Lord, I was not even thinking about You at all."

In my case, I was having a good time going out to the clubs on Friday night, dancing to secular music, smoking cigarettes, and doing many other things too numerous to list. However, the Holy Spirit never stopped wooing me back to the Father, but continued His work, prompting me to stop all this ungodly nonsense and come home to the Father who loves me. Therefore, I say it again, because it bears repeating, it was not I who chose Him, but He who chose me. What a great Father to not leave me to myself, to not leave me with thoughts of pity! It was time to move on and come to the "doing." But if I was to begin to do things for Him, I would first need to learn to abide in Him.

In John 15, the word abide is used ten times. Jesus usually uses a word twice in the same sentence in order to get our attention. But this word abide is used ten times within six verses in this chapter, so He must really want us to understand it. The word abide means "to remain, to stay closely connected, to settle in for the long term." In order to make any type of eternal impact on anyone's life, we need to remain in close connection with God for the long haul. There is no way on this earth that we can do kingdom work without the One to whom the kingdom belongs. Acts 17:28 says it this way: "For in Him we live, and move, and have our being."

RUNNING
HARD AFTER HIM

IF THERE IS ANYTHING I HAVE LEARNED in my sixty-five years of life, it is that God is faithful. One of my favorite passages of Scripture is Lamentations 3:22–23: "Through the Lord's mercies we are not consumed, because His compassions fail not. They are new every morning; great is Your faithfulness." I am a firm believer that God will never fail me. All I have to do is look back over my life at the things He brought me through to see there is no failure in Him. Even in the darkest days of my life, He was there. I can say with the utmost assurance that Jesus is a friend who sticks closer than a brother. He does this because He is on the inside of us. Even family members are limited in what they can do for us, but He is not limited. Our experience of Jesus is limited most often by the limits we put on Him.

I continued to follow hard after Him. I wanted to learn everything I could about Him. In addition to studying the Word of God, I began attending a two-year course hosted by First Church of God in Christ in DeQuincy. This was the Charles Harrison Mason School of Ministry, where we furthered our scriptural knowledge. The very first book we studied gave me greater insight into the God of the universe. We read 2 Timothy 3:16–17, which says, "All Scripture is given by inspiration of God, and is profitable for doctrine, for reproof, for correction, for instruction in righteousness, that the man of God may be complete, thoroughly equipped for every good work." We came to understand that the God who set in place the stars, the sun, and the moon, and who holds them in place, was the same one who inspired mere mortal men by the unction of the Holy Spirit to write the precious words of life found in the Holy Bible. As I have often heard people say, the Bible is our Basic Instruction Before Leaving Earth. We are to live by the words written in His book.

I began to hunger and thirst for more of the Word of God. Psalm 42:1–2 describes how I felt as I began my studies: "As the deer pants for the water brooks, so pants my soul for You, O God. My soul thirsts for God, for the living God." I felt like a sponge as I soaked up everything the instructor gave out at each lesson. I found myself eagerly awaiting each day of school. The classes were at night, so I would get off work and pick up my cousin, who was attending the classes as well, and we would drive to DeQuincy. On the drive home, we would talk about the classes and the things we had learned. It was an awesome time of learning and drawing closer to the Lord.

As I came to a greater understanding of His Word, my faith deepened in the things of God. My spirit man began to grow by leaps and bounds in the knowledge of Jesus Christ, and I understood that is exactly what He wants from each one of us, that our roots would grow deep in Him and we would place all our faith in Him. The Hebrew word for faith is emunah, which means "firmness, steadiness." This word is used to describe the absolute dependability of God's character. Because God is firm and steady, we can put our weight on Him. He is able to carry the weights that so easily beset us, which we were not built to carry anyway. This is why He tells us in 1 Peter 5:7, "Casting all your care upon Him; for He careth for you."

I am learning not to say to people, "Take care." These seem to be harmless-sounding words, and I have spoken them many times when leaving the presence of someone. However, I have learned that we cannot take "care." The definition for care is "the condition of being troubled by fear or worry." And what does the Word tell us about fear? It tells us in 2 Timothy 1:7, "For God hath not given us the spirit of fear; but of power, and of love, and of a sound mind." That being said, we don't want to tell anyone to take care, knowing that it carries with it a spirit of fear, and we certainly do not want them to have to deal with that type of spirit.

The Bible also tells us not to worry, because worry is sin. Worry is an apprehensive or distressed state of mind. The Bible tells us in Matthew 6:34, "Take [do not worry about] therefore no thought for the morrow: for the morrow shall take thought for the things of itself. Sufficient unto the day is the evil thereof." We are to throw down all the things that try to drag us down. As I continued my studies, I learned more and more how to roll all my cares and works upon the Lord because He is trustworthy. Through all those years of unnecessary turmoil, I learned that it is better to trust in God than in yourself, because self will let you down. God, on the other hand, will lift you up.

We continued to study and learn the things of God and eventually finished the course. We completed the two years of study and graduated from the class.

ORDERED STEPS

BY THIS TIME, I HAD LEFT THE WOMEN'S shelter and been hired by Amerisafe, Inc. I began working for Amerisafe on July 1, 1999, and worked there until August 17, 2017, giving eighteen years of service to this company. God planted me in this corporation, and from the very moment I walked through the doors, He advised me that I was on a mission and would not be released until that mission was completed. However, like most people, I did not see the workplace as a mission field because my vision was clouded. All I could see was that I was working for a large corporation, something I had never done before. Consequently, I felt a little intimidated, to say the least. I felt like a small pebble in the large ocean of life. Did I balk against the bit that the Lord had placed in my mouth? Yes, I did! Did it make any difference to God? No, it did not! He had ordered my steps, and they did not change.

I asked God one day why was I there. He told me it was to show the light. Not that I was anything of importance or, as some say, "all that and a bag of chips," but He wanted me to go into that building at 2301 Highway 190 West and allow the light to shine. No matter how I felt that day or what was going on in my life, I was to consistently show the light.

After I settled down and quit fighting against the bit, each day grew a little easier. I understood the real reason I was there: I had a purpose that went beyond just getting a paycheck. That place was my destiny; I was born to be there. Each day I walked through those doors with a smile on my face, even though I may have had a rough night or a rough morning. I was not going to allow that to stop me from being His light. Over the years, I made lots of friends there, some of whom I still remain in contact with, and others are simply carried in my heart. They all will be a part of my life until the day the Lord calls me home because each of them contributed to the maturity in Christ that I gained by knowing them.

I would start my day at 5:00 a.m., getting up early to pray and spend time with the Lord. My time with Him always seemed so short, but I knew that in order to complete the day, I needed to receive His direction and leading. I certainly did not know what to expect from the day, but I knew that He did, and He would not allow me to be ambushed by the enemy.

I once heard someone say that God has ordained everything in heaven and on earth to operate according to a predetermined sequence or order. This is better explained in Romans 8:29–30: "For whom He did foreknow, He also did predestinate to be conformed to the image of His Son, that He might be the firstborn among many brethren. Moreover, whom He did predestinate, them He also called: and whom He called, them He also justified: and whom He justified, them He also glorified."

The word foreknow is the Greek word proginosko, which means "to know beforehand." According to the Dake Annotated Reference Bible, "It is God's plan that He has foreknown and predestinated, and not the individual conformity of free wills to the plan. He has called all men and all are free to accept or reject the call" (emphasis added). This is borne out in John 3:16, which says, "For God so loved the world, that He gave His only begotten Son, that whosoever believeth in Him should not perish, but have everlasting life" (emphasis added). This is further confirmed in 1 Timothy 2:4: "Who will have all men to be saved, and to come unto the knowledge of the truth" (emphasis added); and 2 Peter 3:9: "Whosoever is born of God doth not commit sin; for his seed remains in him; and he cannot sin, because he is born of God" (emphasis added). And lastly, Revelation 22:17 says, "And the Spirit and the bride say, Come. And let him that heareth say, Come. And let him that is athirst come. And whosoever will, let him take the water of life freely" (emphasis added).

All who accept His will, He has foreknown and predestinated to be conformed to the image of His Son that His Son might be the firstborn among many brethren. Those who reject the plan, however, He has foreknown and predestinated to be consigned to eternal hell as an everlasting monument of His wrath on rebels. I don't know about you, but I, for one, do not want to suffer the fate of the latter statement, which comes from rejecting His plan.

I gladly accepted the part I had to play in the kingdom by doing my part in the workplace. I was forty-four years old when I began to work there and stayed until I was sixty-two. Predictably, many changes occurred in my body during this tenure. For example, I began to have problems with my knees. One day when I got up to walk out of the building at the end of the day, I could hardly walk.

I couldn't figure out what in the world had happened. I simply stood up to walk, and my left leg wouldn't cooperate. I managed to limp out of the building.

When I got home, I almost had to crawl out of the car. A few years before, I had suffered a meniscus tear in the right knee, so I had an idea that this might be what was happening with my left knee. Thankfully, the problem occurred on a Friday, so the next day I was able to stay home and rest the knee. However, I could put no weight on the knee.

As I was lying in bed that night, I wondered how to make it to the bathroom. I couldn't crawl, because that would involve using my knees. At just that moment, the Holy Spirit brought to my mind a chair with rollers that was in our bedroom. I hopped on my good leg to the chair, sat down in it, and scooted backward with the good leg into the bathroom. My husband was asleep but awakened to see me maneuvering the chair. "Baby, what is wrong?" he asked. I explained that I had to use the chair to get to the bathroom, so he got up and pushed me to the bathroom and then pushed me back to the bed. I eventually got so used to the chair that I could push myself all the way to the kitchen. I had to maneuver this way for a while until I could get an appointment to see an orthopedist.

When I had the issue with my right knee, the orthopedist had given me a pair of crutches. However, not thinking I would need the crutches again, I had loaned them to a good friend who was having surgery on her foot. Unfortunately, as it turned out, I did need them again, so my husband had to go and get them from her.

I said all that to say this: even though I was in excruciating pain each day at work, I could not allow the pain to make me act any differently with my coworkers or the providers of service that I dealt with on a daily basis. Each day I depended upon the Lord to give me the strength to make it through. He said in His Word in Philippians 4:13, "I can do all things through Christ which strengthened me." I believed that He would give me the strength I needed to make it through, and that is exactly what He did.

One day I was sitting at my desk and received a call from one of my good friends and a sister in Christ. I had had a dream the night before but had not shared it with anyone. In the dream, my husband and I were traveling on a motor home with Elder Jerome Hayes and his wife, Bobbie. It was not clear to whom the motor home belonged, but Elder Hayes was driving. When we stopped for a rest break, there was a man sitting in a chair outside, right beside the motor home. It appeared that he was not feeling well, so my husband placed his hand on the man's head and began to pray, while I put my hand on Larry's back and joined him in prayer. Then I awakened.

Sister Veronica called me and said, "The Lord said to tell you yes," to which I responded, "Yes to what?" She replied, "Yes to the dream you had last night." I could have fallen out of my seat; I was completely shocked because I had not told her about the dream. I realized at that moment that only the Spirit of the living God could have given her that information and then prompted her to call me to confirm the dream's meaning. God will confirm through a person or His Word what He has given you. Through Sister Veronica, God was confirming to me the ministry of healing for my family and me. Furthermore, my good friend Reneé had given a prophetic word that my family and I would be in ministry together. Through both of my friends, the dream was confirmed concerning the ministry to which God was calling my family and me.

This was again confirmed by the many people at the office who called or came to me for prayer. Many times I would stop what I was doing to pray for someone. I believed that if a person asked for prayer, I needed to pray immediately. It was not anything about me, but it was about the God whom I served. I knew Him to be a healer, a deliverer, a provider, and anything else that we need. He is all that and more. I took Him at His word and believed that if I would just pray His Word, He would answer. As Jesus tells us in Matthew 21:22, "And all things, whatsoever ye shall ask in prayer, believing, ye shall receive." We don't have to wonder if we are praying according to His will. If it is in the Word of God and pertains to our situation, then it is His will, because His Word is His will. It is so important that we believe and stay in belief until we see the manifestation of our prayers.

The enemy is busy trying to steal, kill, and destroy our faith. If we are not on guard, he can cause us to miss out on the answer by speaking against the very prayer that we have just prayed. We must keep our conversation in agreement with the expected answer. If after we pray, we begin to talk contrary to what we are expecting, we can miss out on the desired manifestation. This is made plain in James 1:6–8: "But let him ask in faith, nothing wavering, for he that wavereth is like a wave of the sea driven with the wind and tossed. For let not that man think that he shall receive anything of the Lord. A double minded man is unstable in all his ways" (emphasis added). Dake's explains "nothing wavering." It means not doubting, coming from the Greek word diakrino, which means "doubting, staggering." Dake's goes on to explain that he who doubts is like a wave that rises one moment and sinks the next. One minute he believes, and another minute he does not. He says yes and then no to what God has promised, never making up his mind which way he believes. He staggers, helpless in prayer, like a drunken man.

NEVER GIVE UP AND NEVER QUIT!

AS I SAID IN THE BEGINNING OF THIS book, my husband and I have six children together. I have three children by a previous marriage, and he also has three children by a previous marriage. In this portion of the book, I want to talk about my three sons, the three "wise men," as I like to call them. This name may not appear true to those who know them or see them on a daily basis, but this is how God knows them. Many years ago, when my sons were little boys, my cousin Maudie gave me a prayer of consecration, which I prayed over them consistently, night after night. In this prayer, I gave them back to the Lord who blessed me with them. I prayed that He would protect them from danger and cover them with His precious blood.

A few years into our marriage, one of our brothers in Christ, Brother Frost, told my husband to pray for our children, who were teenagers at this time, from Isaiah 54:13–17:

> And all thy children shall be taught of the Lord; and great shall be the peace of thy children. In

righteousness shalt thou be established: thou shalt be far from oppression; for thou shalt not fear: and from terror; for it shall not come near thee. Behold, they shall surely gather together, but not by me: whosoever shall gather together against thee shall fall for thy sake. Behold, I have created the smith that bloweth the coals in the fire, and that bringeth forth an instrument for his work; and I have created the waster to destroy. No weapon that is formed against thee shall prosper; and every tongue that shall rise against thee in judgment thou shalt condemn. This is the heritage of the servants of the Lord, and their righteousness is of me, saith the Lord.

This prayer was also consistently prayed for them.

As I talk about each of my sons, you will see that God does indeed hear and answer prayer. It may not be the way we want, but we have to remember that our Father is sovereign and will do what is best for us. He knows exactly what is best and what needs to be done, but we don't have a clue. I am so grateful to the Lord for how He brought my family and me out with a mighty hand. We are where we are today only because of His grace.

I have recorded a message on my cell phone for others to hear if I am unable to answer. My oldest son used to say, "Momma, your message is too long"; nevertheless, I have kept it on my phone and will continue to do so unless the Lord says something different. Here is the message: "You have reached the voice mailbox of Kathy Taylor. Thank you for calling. I want to leave you a message first. Never let go of your family. I will never let go. I will never let go of my family. I will never let go of God. I will never let go of my faith. I will never let go of the promises that He has given me." So, if you are calling my number and get my message, I pray that you will be blessed by it. Having said that, let's continue with the story of my three "wise men."

HIS BATTLE PLAN

DERRICK E. LYNCH WAS BORN ON MAY 4, 1973. He was a handsome baby boy with the most expressive eyes and a smile to match. He was always in a good mood, smiling a toothless grin all the time. I did my best to take good care of him, so he was contented most of the time.

One day I was sitting outside on the porch swing and he was sitting beside me in his baby seat, smiling his tooth-less grin, when a fly landed on his seat. I snatched up the flyswatter and hit the fly, killing it. It made such a loud noise that it frightened him, and he immediately turned red and let out a squall. You see, I had never raised my voice to him, so he didn't know what all this racket was about. I had to take him out of the seat and hold him until he quieted. And to think that later in his life, when he entered the military, his specialty was field artillery.

I didn't know what to do as a new mother, but one thing I did know was that I wanted my son clean. So I bathed him in the morning and again in the evening before bed-time. As he grew into a young boy, if he went outside and played in the dirt, that meant a bath right then. Each time he got dirty, I bathed him. One day a friend came to visit and noticed how many times I was bathing my son. She laughed and said, "He is a boy—let him be a boy. You don't have to bathe him every minute." With that, I relaxed my bathing vigil. I am sure that he was glad, as those spontaneous baths were likely becoming monotonous to him.

As my son continued to grow, I began to realize that this handsome little boy had his own unique personality. He was kind and caring, but he also had a mind of his own. I was determined to stay one step ahead of him at all times. When he reached the age of five, his father and I separated and divorced. I was pregnant with his brother at the time of the divorce, but that story is for another chapter. After the divorce, I was concerned about this handsome little boy because he loved his father dearly. However, I knew that it was the best thing to do at the time. Unfortunately, I didn't make a good decision long term and ended up in the battle of my life, as I explained in the earlier part of this book.

To say that this did not affect Derrick would not be telling the truth. He was affected in the sense that he became angry as a teenager. I am sure he was angry with me for divorcing his father, although he didn't say it. His acting out, however, told the story. I am so thankful that by this time, I had gotten my head on straight and was living for God. I had a personal relationship with Him and trusted that all things would work out in my son's life. My faith in God was what brought me through. Faith is "the leaning of your whole personality on God in complete trust and confidence." Even though I didn't have all the answers, I had peace, knowing that God would heal my son's emotions in time. Everything happens in God's timing.

When Derrick reached the twelfth grade, he decided that he wanted to go to summer school and graduate later. Thank God for the Holy Spirit that will never lead you wrong. I knew that if Derrick did not graduate in May, he was not going to graduate. He was not going to go to summer school and would become a high school dropout.

Derrick was having difficulty in his English class, so I started meeting with his teacher. I got his assignments, and when he came home from school, we would go over the assignments together. We did this every day, and his grades improved to the point that he passed his English class. Thank the Lord, he graduated from high school. This was a strenuous time for me because it took place during the time I was recovering from the hysterectomy and the cancer treatments. But I knew God would give me the strength that I needed to help my son make it through and graduate, and He did just that. God is such a good, good Father!

On the day he graduated, he went to live with his father that night. From there he entered the military, where he had a good career until the sixteenth year. Then things began to go wrong. Derrick had completed two back-to-back overseas tours, one to Afghanistan and the other to Bosnia. He had also been deployed to Korea on a twelve-month tour. During the time he was stationed in Hawaii, he called me one day to say it felt as if something was wrong, but he didn't know what it was. By this time, he had married a woman in the military that he had met in Korea, and they had a daughter.

If you never face trials, you will never have to exercise your faith. My faith was now being tested concerning this problem with Derrick. I continued to receive calls from my son and began to feel in my spirit that I needed to go to him in Hawaii. This feeling was further heightened by a telephone call I received from Celestine, Derrick's wife. During this phone call, the Lord impressed upon me to book a flight to Hawaii.

I had never flown before and was talking with my sister Brenda about my feelings. She, however, had flown several times and decided to fly with me to Hawaii so I wouldn't be alone and she could help me with the layovers. I was so glad to have her with me, so off we flew to Hawaii. We knew this was a "mission" trip. We weren't going to sightsee or to enjoy the multitude of fantastic events that I am sure Derrick and Celestine would have provided for us if things had been different. Both my sister and I knew the real reason we were there.

As the plane touched down and we were preparing to disembark, I developed a severe earache. I had been chewing gum as advised by my sister but still had the most unbearable pain imaginable. As we lined up to get off the plane, I told my sister about it; I couldn't figure out what in the world was going on. As we entered the terminal, the pain subsided and went away just as quickly as it began. That is when I knew I was under attack by the enemy. He knew the reason I was there and wanted to discourage me from the plan the Lord had given me, but it was not going to work. I knew what God had said I should do, and I was not going to allow the enemy to deter me from it.

Celestine picked us up and drove us to their home; Derrick was unable to come with her. Celestine had told us earlier that Derrick was unable to leave the house for any length of time. He had not even been able to go to work. Thankfully, his company commander was willing to work with him and allowed Derrick to go to work and then return home after roll call.

Let me interject something here that was strategically given to me by one of my good friends and sisters in Christ, Tammy Foote. After I returned home, I talked with her about my son's situation, and this is what she said the Lord had given her. I wanted to share this because sometimes we don't realize what kinds of battles we may have to go through in life, but we must always remember that God knows everything about our situations and is not surprised about anything that happens. Tammy gave me this scripture from Luke 2:23 in the Amplified Bible: "As it is written in the Law of the Lord, Every [firstborn] male that opens the womb shall be set apart and dedicated and called holy to the Lord." Tammy explained that there is something significant about the first; in the Bible, the first harvest, the firstfruits, and the firstborn of the livestock were the Lord's. She said she didn't fully understand it, but there was indeed a significance.

As I studied this, I found a second scripture in Exodus 13:2 that said something similar: "Sanctify unto me all the firstborn, whatsoever openeth the womb among the children of Israel, both of man and of beast: it is Mine." The word sanctify in the Hebrew is qadash, which means "to set apart from a profane to a sacred purpose." This is not a reference to cleansing from sin or removal of what is commonly called "the old man." Here it refers to the setting apart of the firstborn of both man and beast for holy uses. This is not to say that all the other children are not as important and as special as the first. I simply want to show just how hard the enemy fights the firstborn son in a family. The enemy hates God, so anything or anyone that God refers to as being dedicated to Him will have to go through the fire and contend with the onslaught of the devil. Remember, however, that God is still in control, and He does not slumber or sleep. He knows every step of the way and how things are going to turn out.

Having said that, let me go back to Derrick. The Lord had prompted me to pray every day we were there. In obedience to that directive, I would get up around 5:00 a.m. and go sit in their living room to read the Bible and pray. Toward the end of our visit, Celestine, who had been on a military training event in California, had to go pick up Aniya, their daughter, who was living with her mother in New York at the time. Consequently, she would not be able take us back to the airport when our flight was scheduled to depart.

Each day of our visit, Derrick would get up and prepare all our meals, even to the point of dishing out our plates, so we didn't have to do anything. I thanked God for that. At various points throughout the day, he would say, "Mom, let's have Bible study." That was right up my alley, as I loved to study the Word of God and expound on it, so the three of us would study and have prayer afterward.

We were there for five days. The day before our last day, my sister said that she had lain down to take a nap, and before drifting off to sleep, she saw a dark form flow through the room and out the window. I knew then that the enemy's hold had been broken! The Word of God tells us to "submit yourselves therefore to God, resist the devil, and he will flee from you." I had submitted myself to the Lord by following His Word and praying each day. I had resisted the devil by not going back to sleep in the mornings, but getting up with determination, knowing this was my son's life that was at stake. The devil had no other recourse but to get out of there.

On the fifth day of our visit, November 2, 2007, I wrote this in my journal to the Lord:

I begin this journal entry with heartfelt thanks to You, Lord, for all You have done, for all You are doing, and for all You are going to do. I am believing and standing on Your word that "the struggle is over." The journey was painful but was a necessary part of the preparation. Through the journey God taught the Israelites who He was: the living God, the leader of their nation, and this is who is teaching my son. During this time of quiet, Derrick's God is being made known to him. God is clearing up any misconceptions Derrick may have had in the past, and He is making clear to Derrick His great love for him—a love that will never fail, a love that is deeper and wider than any ocean or any sea. I, as his mother, yield my rights to You. I step aside so that You can do what is best for my son, because I realize that only You know what is absolutely best for him. This spiritual pilgrimage may be lengthy, and he may face pain, discouragement, and difficulties; but always in the forefront of my mind will be this knowing that God isn't just trying to keep him alive; He wants to prepare Derrick to live in service and devotion to Him.

On the day of our departure, Derrick was able to leave the house and take us to the airport. This was a big step forward for him, because he had not been able to do that before we came. I give God all the glory!

As I end this chapter, God is still preparing him. However, I know in my "knower" that what the Word of God says in Philippians 1:6, "Being confident of this very thing that He which hath begun a good work in you [Derrick] will perform it until the day of Jesus Christ," is true. On this word I will stand until the complete and total manifestation comes to pass.

GREATER GRACE

AS I WAS PREPARING TO WRITE THIS chapter about my middle son, Darrius Omar Lynch, Sr., I pulled out a book from my bookcase by Max Lucado titled In the Grip of Grace. Inscribed on the inside of the jacket cover were these words: "To: Mrs. Kathy Taylor; From: Mr. and Mrs. Omar Lynch. Enjoy! We love you!" As I read the inside of the book cover, I just had to insert the following words from Mr. Lucado to this part of my book. I hope he won't mind.

Can anything separate us from the love Christ has for us? Does God really love us forever? Not just on Easter Sunday when our shoes are shined and our hair is fixed. We want to know, how does God feel about me when I mess up, fail, or fall short? When I snap at anything that moves, when my thoughts are gutter-level; when my tongue is sharp enough to slice a rock. How does He feel about me then? That's the question. Can I drift too far? Wait too long? Slip too much? Did I out-sin the love of God? The answer is found in one of life's sweetest words—GRACE!

Darrius Omar Lynch, Sr., was born on January 23, 1978. He slid into the world with a fluid motion that took all of us by surprise. I was supposed to have an epidural, but by the time they got me to the delivery room, this anxious little boy was already making his grand entrance. Impetuous was the word for this little bundle of joy, and it still describes him today. He came in making his mark on the world, and everything he did after that had to be done quick, fast, and in a hurry. He did not stop to think about things before rushing headlong into action, unlike his younger brother who would come after him (but that is another chapter). We decided to call him by his middle name, Omar. There wasn't time to call him anything longer than that because he could move in a flash and be out the door before you finished saying his first name. So Omar it was.

This was the one son who reminded me so much of myself. I am sure that the enemy must have taken a look at him and said, "Oh no, we've got to do something with him right now. We cannot let him get ahead of us and discover his identity, because if he does, we will be defeated on every hand." So the enemy began to war with this little boy, and the little boy who jumped out of the womb as if to say, "Okay, here I am—take your best shot," found himself in a battle.

Around the age of two months, Omar developed asthma. He would begin to sweat profusely, his temperature would rise, and off we would go to the hospital. You could hear the rattle inside his chest as he labored to breathe. The hospital personnel would do all of the preliminaries and then place him under a mist tent, where he would spend the majority of his time during his stay in the hospital. Just from looking at him, you would have never thought he was as sickly as he was. Even at this young age, he had a muscular physique, as if he had been lifting weights while inside my body. There was no fat on his body—he was all lean. I imagine his future athletic abilities could be attributed to this, because he excelled in any type of sports that he undertook.

Not only did Omar have asthma to contend with, but he also was born with a protruding navel. It was so large that when he coughed, it looked as if it would explode. This made me very nervous, since he coughed a lot as a result of his respiratory issues. I therefore talked with his primary doctor about the possibility of surgery. He referred us to a doctor in Lake Charles who performed the surgery. I did not want him to go through many more years like that, and thankfully, it was done before he started school. As you know, children can be so cruel.

This impetuous little boy began Happy Day Head Start at the age of three. Every day he would bring something home from his lunch for his younger brother. They were only two years apart in age and were very close. At that time, my mother was taking care of them, since I was employed at the welfare office. One day at work, I received a call from the director of the Head Start program, Mrs. Pierce. She informed me that Omar had crossed the road to go to the playground where he saw his older brother, Derrick, playing. Mrs. Pierce decided he was too young to attend school and suggested we wait another year for him to gain more maturity.

I laugh every time I think how he was expelled from Head Start. She was right, though; he needed more time to grow emotionally. The scars he received from those years when I struggled from abuse took a toll on him emotionally. It would be many years and require much prayer and unconditional love before he would shake the demons that hounded him. But I did not give up on him then and will not ever give up on my son.

Omar tried to mask his feelings of unworthiness by taking drugs, and sadly, this began at an early age. The drugs made him feel like the person he felt he should have been. He didn't understand that he was a person of worth. The enemy of his soul kept him blind to the truth of who he really was for a very long time.

I will never forget the word of prophecy concerning Omar that my good friend Reneé Abshire gave me. At the time of the prophetic word, I did not know her and had never seen her before. She came to the church I was attending in order to sing a song. After the service was over, she asked if she could pray for me. I agreed to the prayer. She prayed for me and my family and said that the Lord told her to tell me who Omar was. She said the Lord gave her this scripture from Isaiah 11:1–5:

> And there shall come forth a rod out of the stem of Jesse, and a Branch shall grow out of his roots: And the spirit of the Lord shall rest upon him, the spirit of wisdom and understanding, the spirit of counsel and might, the spirit of knowledge and of the fear of the Lord; and shall make him of quick understanding in the fear of the Lord: and he shall not judge after the sight of his eyes, neither reprove after the hearing of his ears. But with righteousness shall he judge the poor, and reprove with equity for the meek of the earth: and he shall smite the earth with the rod of his mouth, and with the breath of his lips shall he slay the wicked. And righteousness shall be the girdle of his loins, and faithfulness the girdle of his reins.

I needed to hear this because Omar would go through many hard things, and many wounds would pierce him through. Many people would not understand him and why he was doing the things he did. But God knew, and God wanted me to know so that I would not ever give up on him, never turn my back on him, so that his change could come.

You see, there is a due time for everyone on this earth. My time is not like your time, and neither is your time like mine. Everyone has their own set time for change. So every time I would think, Okay, God, I don't see how this is going to turn out, He would remind me not to focus on the actions being displayed, but to remember who Omar really was. Each time I couldn't understand how some situation was going to work out, God intervened and brought him through it.

I firmly believe it is the anointing that destroys the yoke of bondage. It is the power of God that grants the ability to perform the purpose that God has ordained for each born-again believer to accomplish while here on planet Earth. It is the reason we were sent here by way of our mothers' wombs. No one can fulfill my purpose in life, and likewise, I cannot fulfill anyone else's purpose. We all have a divine purpose. If you don't yet know yours, search God and find out why you were born. Don't continue to aimlessly wander through life. Do as Paul told Timothy in 2 Timothy 1:6: "Wherefore I put thee in remembrance that thou stir up the gift of God, which is in thee by the putting on of my hand."

God deals with me in dreams and visions. Throughout the years, I have had many dreams and visions concerning this child of mine. God showed me these things ahead of time so that I would pray, first of all, and also so that

I would continue to hold to the visions He had given me. Otherwise, in the days of adversity, I might faint, because some of the things this child traveled through were very hard. I am only going to share one of the myriad things that he went through, so as not to take up space in the book for other things that need to be said.

Saying that, let me share one dream the Lord gave me in 2013, which I didn't understand at first. However, when the events began to manifest sometime later, the Lord spoke to me and said, This is the dream I gave you.

The dream began with me being in my mother's home on Rock Street. I was sitting in the living room, and others were there too, but I didn't recognize them. Next to the living room was the bedroom where my mother slept. Out of this room people began to emerge—three men to be exact—and one them was Brad Pitt. It seemed that the other two men were doing a job for Brad, but one of them was not wholehearted in his performance. Suddenly Brad began to beat this man unmercifully. The beating began in the living room and continued into another bedroom, the one next to my mother's room. As he beat the man, who by this time was lying on his back in the bed, everyone in the house gathered in the room to watch, but no one stopped him, at least not for several minutes. Finally, someone pulled Brad off the beaten man, and remarkably, there was no blood anywhere on his face or body. It was as if he had not been beaten at all. It was unbelievable. I could not understand how he could have taken such a beating and the results of the attack not be visible. I would soon find out the reason.

About two weeks later, Omar called me at work to ask if I would stop by his place after work, saying that he needed to show me something that was bothering him.

When I got there, he showed me a knot on the lower part of his back, and it was very painful. I told him he needed to go to the ER and let them check this out. He did so, and I went with him. The ER attendant ran some blood tests, and the results showed that his kidneys were failing. The hospital in the town we lived in did not have a dialysis room, so they had to send him to Rapides General Hospital in Alexandria, Louisiana. He was transported by ambulance that very night, and I told him I would be there in the morning.

Our youngest son took me to see him the following day. The hospital personnel had begun to run the necessary tests. I perceived in my spirit that I needed to stay, so after calling my husband, I told my youngest son to go back without me. I wanted to be there to speak with the doctor when he made his rounds.

When the doctor made his rounds that evening, he expressed concern about the distress that the kidneys were in. He informed me that Omar had suffered a heatstroke, and the kidneys had suffered tremendously from it. He was on strong antibiotics, but the doctor kept saying he needed to insert a catheter. Both Omar and I didn't understand what he meant by the catheter, assuming it was a catheter for draining urine from the bladder, and Omar didn't want this tubing in his body.

The next day, when the doctor came into the room, I asked him about the catheter, and he explained that it was a catheter for dialysis. Because the kidneys were not working, the doctors needed access in order to dialyze him. I understood then what he was saying and explained this to Omar, who immediately agreed to the procedure. Thank the Lord, I was prompted to get the doctor to further clarify, because time is of the essence when you are dealing with kidney failure. The procedure was performed, and dialysis was begun. I stayed several days, but finally I had to return home and to work.

When I was able to take off again, I returned to the hospital. The doctors wanted to put in another line for the dialysis, this time in his chest area, as the original line had been placed in his neck. The second line would be a more permanent line. He was scheduled for this procedure, and it was completed without any issues.

Each day I was there, I would pray and anoint his room. On the days when they took him for dialysis, I was able to pray aloud. There was a board in the room that listed the nurse's information, the room number, the doctor's information, and other pertinent facts. A space was left where the patient could write what they wanted to see happen during their stay. In this blank space, I wrote this scripture: "Beloved, I wish above all things that thou mayest prosper and be in health, even as thy soul prospereth" (3 John 2). You see, it is God's will that we prosper in spirit, soul, and body. I believed this scripture was saying what needed to happen, so every day I was there, I would declare this word out loud. I encouraged my son to say this word out loud when I was not there so that his body could hear what his mouth was speaking and come in line with it.

One day while I was there, a visitor knocked on Omar's door, accompanied by another person. Neither my son nor I had ever seen these two men before. The visitor introduced himself as a pastor at a local church and said he often ministered at the hospital. The young man who accompanied him was a minister in the same church. The pastor said that the Lord had directed him to Omar's room. He was getting ready to leave the hospital when the Lord said to him, You are not finished yet. There is someone else you need to see. He didn't know who the someone was, but he turned around and got back on the elevator, coming up to the floor where we were. He didn't know which room he was to enter, he said, but as he walked past Omar's door, he was led to turn around. He then knocked on the door, and we invited him in.

I actually had noticed him and the young man when they passed the door, because the door was open enough to see into the hallway. The pastor entered the room and introduced himself and the minister. We introduced ourselves, and he began to speak with Omar. At one point in his ministering, he began to speak prophetically to Omar. He told him that he (Omar) had a call on his life from the Lord, but he had been running from it. He said that he needed to answer the call. I knew what he was saying was the truth, because the Lord had already spoken that same word to me. Omar, too, knew this to be the truth. As the pastor continued to minister, tears began to flow as Omar listened to what was being said to him. This pastor ministered for several minutes, then advised us that his work was completed and left the room. We were both in amazement at how the Lord had confirmed His word to Omar.

On November 16, 2013, my sister Annie Marie gave me a scripture for Omar: "I have therefore whereof I may glory through Jesus Christ in those things which pertain to God.... Through mighty signs and wonders, by the power of the Spirit of God" (Rom. 15:17, 19). It was followed by this short prayer: Father, thank You for the mighty signs and wonders that You are showing us. We thank You for the lowering of the creatinine in Omar's blood to the level of one or below. On this same day, this word was also given to me: "Something significant will begin to happen on November 20. Expect to see a greater release of God's power, presence, revelation, and healing."

On November 20, I was sitting in the study when the telephone rang. It was Omar, and he sounded so excited He said, "Ma, my kidneys have begun to function! I was sitting in the chair in the room and almost didn't make it to the bathroom in time. They began to flow!" He said one of the nurses had told him that one of the signs that his kidneys were functioning again would be an abundance of urine. And sure enough, Omar said, as soon as he finished, he needed to go back to the bathroom only five minutes later. When we finished the conversation, I began to praise the Lord. I knew this was the manifestation of the word He had given my sister, along with prayer. Not to say that there were not others who were praying for him. All our family members were praying, along with our church members, others in the community, and others that I didn't even know about.

On the following Monday, Omar called again and said they were getting ready to release him from the hospital but wanted to put in a permanent access so he could have dialysis upon release. But first, they would look at his lab work and then make a determination about what was needed. He called back a little later to say there was no need for permanent access because the creatinine level was below one, and the kidneys were functioning adequately, cleansing the blood as is their function.

When he said that, the Lord reminded me of the dream about the man having no blood anywhere on him after receiving a terrible beating. It was God in the dream who pulled Brad Pitt off the man, and the man who had been beaten was Omar. I think Brad Pitt was the man in my dream because of a movie he had made many years ago,

Meet Joe Black. If you remember, he portrayed death in that movie. I think, by the continual beating in the dream, the Lord was showing me how much the enemy wanted to kill Omar. But just as He stopped the fight in the dream, He stopped the fight in Omar's life, and Omar did not look like what he had been through. Only God can do a thing like that!

HOLY SPIRIT COVERING

NOW I COME TO THE THIRD SON THE
Lord blessed me with. Ordonis Ali Lynch (Bubba is what
we affectionately call him) was born on January 24, 1980.
I thought he would be born on the same date as his brother
Omar, but it didn't work out that way. It was not meant to
be—Bubba needed his own birth date. He was his own
person in his own right, so very different from his brothers.
I went into labor with him on the twenty-third, which was
Omar's birth date, but did not have him until the evening
of the following day. It was a very hard labor, almost as if
he were trying to tell me, "I don't want to come out of this
safe place inside your womb, Momma. Just let me stay
here a little while longer."

The doctor gave an order to induce labor; I thought this
would make things easier after all the pain I had already
endured. Little did I know, however, that inducing labor
would actually make the pain more intense. By the time
the doctor got to the hospital, I caught his hand and said,
"Where have you been? You need to help me!"

I guess he had heard that many times before from young
mothers with long labors, because he sort of chuckled

and said, "Okay, I am here now. It won't be much longer." True to his word, a few agonizing minutes later, Bubba was born. He was a beautiful baby with long eyelashes and a head full of curly dark hair. I took one look at him and forgot all about the long labor I had just endured. I understand clearly the scripture in John 16:21 that says "a woman when she is in travail hath sorrow, because her hour is come; but as soon as she is delivered of the child, she remembereth no more the anguish, for joy that a man is born into the world." What a joy he was then, and continues to be!

I actually did not give Ali the nickname of Bubba; I didn't give any of my boys a nickname. The neighborhood children began to call him Bubba, and it just sort of stuck. Bubba was the child who believed everything I said. He took at face value that if his momma said something, it must be true. He did not question it. Needless to say, he did not get as many whippings as his brothers. In fact, I hated to whip Bubba, mainly because he screamed so loudly you would think he was being killed. He would even begin to scream at the mere mention of a whipping. Rather than go through all that murderous noise, I would talk to him or punish him in a different way. That worked better for me too, because I didn't like having to whip my little boy.

What a sense of humor this little boy had! He loved to laugh, and his older brother Omar, who was the jokester of the house, knew how to keep him laughing. It seemed that everything Omar said was funny to Bubba. There was never a dull moment when those two were in the house. Bubba was the one of my three children who took education seriously. He was an A student from the first grade and into high school. I did not have to worry about whether or not he had homework or completed it, because if he did have homework, he did it soon as he got home from school. He was the child who was excited to let me know the day report cards would be sent home. I am sure his brothers were not too thrilled with his announcement, but they had no choice, since Bubba would tell me as soon as I got home from work.

Just as he was excited about secular education, Bubba was also excited about the spiritual. At the age of eight, he gave his life to the Lord and received salvation. He was so excited and wanted everyone to know that he was part of the kingdom of God. He was just as conscientious about Sunday school as he was about doing his homework. He wanted to be there on time, and whatever his Sunday school teacher told him, he was sure it was the gospel truth.

Bubba continued in this pattern until he reached high school, and then things began to slowly take a different turn. He was so naïve that he thought everyone was like him, honest and trustworthy, that they did what they said they would do. Sadly, he soon discovered that was not the way of the world. First Corinthians 15:33 warns us, "Be not deceived: evil communications corrupt good manners." As Bubba began to follow the crowd, things began to spiral downward for him. He no longer possessed the same enthusiasm for school that he had as a young boy. His lessons were not completed, his grades declined, and my once naïve little boy was sucked into a whirlwind of captivity.

At the age of eighteen, Bubba got into serious trouble and ended up incarcerated for four years. It was so hard to watch him struggle through those years of being away from his family. He was now the father of two beautiful daughters, whom he loved dearly. I would take them to visit him, and I know he didn't enjoy them seeing him in this situation. Nevertheless, I am so thankful to Jesus that He watched over him and protected him throughout those years.

Bubba told me many years later that as he was on the prison bus being transported to the facility, he realized how serious his situation was. He knew he had to make a decision at that moment, and the decision he made would affect him for the rest of his life. Thanks be to God, he made the right decision! He turned to the only one who could offer him the help he needed at that time. Just as Hezekiah in 2 Kings 20:2 "turned his face to the wall, and prayed unto the Lord," Bubba turned his face to the window of that bus and cried out to the Lord, repenting of all the wrong he had done up to that point in his young life. What he didn't realize was that the Lord had not turned His back on him. He had known where he was every moment and was just waiting for him to turn back to Him. In fact, He knew that Bubba would eventually turn back to the God who loved him so much that He gave His life for him.

When he reached the facility, he wrote me a long letter, apologizing for the wrong decisions that had led him there. I was so happy to hear that he had repented to the Lord and was forgiven. God had wiped the slate clean, and he could go forward, this time with the Lord at the head of his life again. And believe me, he never turned back again. He has continued to walk with the Lord. Is he perfect? No. No one is perfect. But he continues to strive for the perfection that one day will be for all of us when Jesus comes to claim His bride, the church, in the rapture.

During the time Bubba was away, he wrote many letters to me. How I looked forward to each one! My heart was made glad with each word I read. In one of his letters, he shared the words the Lord had spoken to him from Scripture concerning the call He had placed upon his life. Jeremiah 1:5–10 reads:

> Before I formed thee in the belly I knew thee; and before thou camest forth out of the womb I sanctified thee, and I ordained thee a prophet unto the nations. Then said I, Ah Lord God! Behold, I cannot speak: for I am a child. But the Lord said unto me [Ordonis], Say not, I am a child: for thou shalt go to all that I shall send thee, and whatsoever I command thee thou shalt speak. Be not afraid of their faces: for I am with thee to deliver thee, saith the Lord. Then the Lord put forth His hand, and touched my mouth, and the Lord said unto me [Ordonis], Behold, I have put my words in thy mouth. See, I have this day set thee over the nations and over the kingdoms, to root out, and to pull down, and to destroy, and to throw down, to build, and to plant.

The Lord gave this passage to Bubba even though he was far away from his family and had veered off the path God had for him. However, by God's grace and mercy, he had returned to the one who loved him more than death itself. He let Bubba know that he had been chosen while still in my womb for a work that only he could accomplish. God knew Bubba. He approved of him; He sanctified or set him apart; He ordained or commissioned him before he was born. God knew that he was going to veer off the path; that was no surprise to Him. But He also knew that he would get back on the path again and not allow this setback to keep him in captivity.

It is one thing to be in captivity, but it is another thing to stay there. Bubba did just as the prodigal son did in Luke 15:17: "And when he came to himself, he said, How many hired servants of my father's have bread enough and to spare, and I perish with hunger!" (emphasis added). The condition that Bubba was in made him realize there had to be a change in his life, and that change had to be made right then. He made the immediate decision to repent, but he knew that making a decision alone wasn't enough; he had to be sincere and genuine in his acts, words, and deeds. He thus followed it up with getting baptized, even though no one in the family was there to support him as he went under the water.

It was only he and the Lord there, but that was okay. God was the one who was taking care of him, protecting him from dangers we knew nothing about, watching over him, giving him favor, and answering his prayers. He was letting Bubba know that as long as he stayed on His side, he would not lack any good thing. To this day, God has done just that. He has blessed Bubba over and over again. He travels all over this state and other states with a softball team named Fury, which he and his wife, Lisa, coach together. He is pouring into these young lives the understanding that if you put God first, there is nothing you cannot do. It matters not how young or old a person is—we all need the Savior.

TRUE PEACE

ALEXANDER MACLAREN HAS SAID, "TRUE peace comes not from the absence of trouble, but from the Presence of God, and will be deep and passing all understanding in the exact measure in which we live in and partake of the love of God." I have found that statement to be true. Peace does not come automatically, but rather, we have to make a decision to yield to peace in order for it to manifest in our lives. After that, we must further decide not to yield to anxiety and fear.

The enemy wants us to believe that God is not going to answer our prayers, maybe because of some errors we have made in our lives. The enemy tries to hold things over our heads in order to move us out of faith and into fear. Nevertheless, we must pray in faith, believing that we receive what we are praying about, and then the peace of God results. That peace, His peace, will slam the door on anxiety and fear every time. This is because that peace does not belong to us—it is His peace.

Colossians 3:15 in the Amplified Bible says, "Let the peace (soul harmony which comes) from Christ rule (act as umpire continually) in your hearts [deciding and settling with finality all questions that arise in your minds, in that peaceful state] to which as [members of Christ's] one body you were also called [to live]" (emphasis added). You see, Jesus is the Prince of Peace; He is the Source of true peace. His Word tells us so in John 14:27: "Peace I leave with you, my peace I give unto you: not as the world giveth, give I unto you. Let not your heart be troubled, neither let it be afraid" (emphasis added).

This was Jesus' dying legacy to us—peace. Certainly, it is not like the peace the world offers. Nations make peace treaties but still arm themselves for war, even as they continue calling for peace. Man is so fickle in his dealings. He can be at peace today and at war tomorrow. But thanks be to our almighty God! He is not wishy-washy.

Let me move on now to a testimony concerning my husband. I retired on August 17, 2017, not knowing that at the end of that year, a situation would come into our lives that would shake us to the core. God, of course, knew what was going to happen and was not shaken by the turn of events.

On December 17, 2017, while my husband lay in Beauregard Memorial Hospital, God gave me this word from Isaiah 41:10 in the Amplified Bible: "Fear not (there is nothing to fear), for I am with you; do not look around you in terror and be dismayed, for I am your God. I will strengthen and harden you to difficulties, yes, I will help you; yes, I will hold you up and retain you with My (victorious) right hand of rightness and justice. For I the Lord your God will hold your right hand; I am the Lord, Who says to you, Fear not; I will help you!" I would have to learn to cling to that promise as I learned the full extent of what lay ahead.

FAITH TESTED BY FIRE

SECOND CORINTHIANS 4:16-18 SAYS,
"Therefore we do not lose heart. Even though our outward man is perishing, yet our inward man is being renewed day by day. For our light affliction, which is but for a moment, is working for us a far more exceeding and eternal weight of glory, while we do not look at the things which are seen, but at the things which are not seen. For the things which are seen are temporary, but the things which are not seen are eternal."

As I put to paper this testimony of God's faithfulness and unconditional love, I am amazed at His leading and guiding from the very beginning of this storm. It is easy to say, as many of us do, "God is in control," but when you are the one in a situation of great magnitude, those words take on special meaning. I am not trying to imply that I am more than anyone else. I am sure many, possibly thousands, of people have gone through situations of even greater magnitude. Nonetheless, God has given me these words to share with the world what He can do if we put our total trust in Him when our backs are against the wall. The Bible says, "For the eyes of the Lord run to and fro throughout the whole earth, to shew Himself strong in the behalf of them whose heart is perfect toward Him" (2 Chron. 16:9). The word perfect in the Hebrew is shalem, which means "full, just, made ready, peaceable, quiet." As Christians, we are grateful to be vessels that show God strong in our lives.

In the early part of December 2017, God gave me a dream. In this dream, Larry and I were in a crowd of people at what seemed to be a picnic, since it was outside. Everyone was laughing and having a good time. We prepared to leave, but as we were walking away from the crowd, a door appeared. As we walked toward this door, I reached out to open it, and just as I did that, Larry's right hip joined to my left hip. I looked at him and laughed, saying, "What are you doing?" and then I awakened. Little did I know that Larry and I were about to embark on a journey, and from this journey, we would not return the same.

Sometime earlier, Larry had begun to not feel well. He was fatigued all the time, so we were not able to attend church as much as we had before. In fact, most Sundays we were at one of the urgent care clinics in our area. On Wednesday, December 6, 2017, the Lord impressed me to call Dr. Pandya, Larry's primary care physician, and ask him to order some X-rays of Larry's chest. He had been having quite a few infections; as soon as he recovered from one, two weeks later he would be sick again. Dr. Pandya agreed to my request, so on the following day, Larry and I went to the local hospital for the X-rays, then went home after the completion of the tests.

I later called Dr. Pandya's office to see if they had the results. I was prompted by the Holy Spirit that time was of the essence. When I could not reach the office personnel by phone, I told Larry, "I am going into town to Dr.

Pandya's office." This was on a Thursday, and on Friday, the office was normally closed. I knew that if I didn't act now upon the Holy Spirit's leading, I would not get any results until next week. However, when I got to the doctor's office, it was closed. I sat in the parking lot and said, "Lord, I don't know what to do. Please help me. Tell me what to do now." The Lord said, Go across the road and back to the hospital, and find the radiology tech that did the X-rays. I did what He said.

When I got to the radiology area, the tech had her purse on her arm, preparing to leave for the day. I asked if I could speak with her for a moment, and I explained my situation. I told her all I needed was an explanation of the results. She agreed to give me a copy of the report and suggested I take this copy across the street to the urgent care clinic and ask the nurse practitioner to provide an explanation of the findings. When I got to the urgent care, the receptionist said yes, they could give an explanation, but Larry would have to be with me. I went back home, but Larry did not feel well enough to return to the clinic with me, so there was nothing more to be done that day.

The next day was Friday, and we went to the urgent care facility. We waited for about two hours, and then instead of calling Larry's name, they called me to the back, where the receptionist said that the nurse practitioner did not feel comfortable giving us the results, and that we should go to the hospital and let a doctor go over the findings. I explained that we had already waited two hours and Larry was not feeling well, so she said she would call ahead to the hospital ER and explain our situation, and they would take us right in to triage. True to her word, she called, and when we got there, they immediately took us back to see the doctor.

The doctor soon came into the room and asked why we were there, so I explained about needing the X-ray results. He evidently had already looked at the X-rays, because he began talking about lesions on the lung walls. None of this made any sense to me at the time, because in my mind I was thinking this was some type of viral infection. I am sure he saw the confusion on my face, so he said he would call Dr. Pandya.

Soon a nurse brought me a telephone with Dr. Pandya on the line. Dr. Pandya explained that he was ordering a CT scan of Larry's chest, an injection in his stomach because his calcium level was extremely high, and a complete blood workup. When these results returned, another ER doctor came and said, "We are admitting your husband to the hospital immediately. His calcium level is sixteen, an extremely high level." This doctor further advised that he would notify Dr. Pandya of the situation. With that, we went upstairs and were settled into a room.

This marked the first day of our stay in Beauregard Memorial Hospital. On the second day of this stay, December 9, 2017, the Lord gave me the words I previously stated. We were to stay five days in the hospital. On Tuesday, December 12, 2017, I asked Dr. Pandya to transfer Larry to Lake Charles, since the doctors could not determine the source of a recurring evening fever Larry had each day. Dr. Pandya agreed with my request and immediately began the transfer paperwork to Christus St. Patrick Hospital in Lake Charles. Not only did he prepare the paperwork for the transfer, but he went one step further and arranged for four doctors to take care of Larry during his stay.

We traveled by ambulance to the hospital in Lake Charles and arrived there in the early hours of the morning, where we were placed on the fifth floor. Blood was drawn each day and tests were run. Not until the very last test was completed, which was a bone marrow biopsy, would the doctors be able to make a conclusive diagnosis. All the other tests had showed nothing.

It was Christmas Eve, and we were released to go home. We thus had to wait through the holidays for the results of the biopsy. Needless to say, we did not exchange any gifts that year. We were so thankful just to be together for one more Christmas that we did not even think about that part of the holiday. We thanked the Lord at every opportunity as we awaited the biopsy results.

On January 2, 2018, Dr. Pandya called and informed us that the bone marrow biopsy tested positive for multiple myeloma, a cancer of the bone marrow plasma. He asked Larry's permission to call M. D. Anderson Hospital in Houston, Texas, saying he would call them as soon as he finished speaking with us. We thank the Lord for Dr. Pandya's rapid response, because we had no idea how far along the cancer was or how far it might have spread. We soon received a call from M. D. Anderson and was given an appointment for January 9, 2018. I was amazed at how quickly the appointment had been scheduled. The scheduler advised us to prepare to remain in Texas from the ninth through the twelfth of January, as Larry would have to undergo a battery of tests each day in order for the doctors to develop a treatment plan.

We made preparations for the trip. Our son Ali (Bubba) and his wife, Lisa, drove us to Houston, where we would stay from that Tuesday until Friday. Larry was very weak, but he managed to walk to each appointment in the hospital. M. D. Anderson is huge; we were not used to having to get on elevators and go to different clinics within the hospital. We would sometimes get lost, but the Lord always had someone there to see our perplexed faces and either give us directions or walk with us to the place where we needed to be. That's just one more example of God's mercy and favor. When we finished the tests for each day, we went back to our motel room, where Larry would eat and immediately go to sleep.

After all the tests were completed, our daughter-in-law Celestine picked us up on the twelfth and drove us home to Louisiana. Everything was going well, until that Sunday morning of January 14, 2018. Larry ate breakfast but had problems keeping the food down. After breakfast, he lay back down and slept. Later in the morning, I gave him a glass of Sprite, thinking it would settle his stomach. It actually did stay down, and he again went to sleep. Later in the day, I gave him a tangerine, just to see if it would stay down. It did not. I noticed that as he slept, he made strange noises, and additionally, his voice began to sound unusual. He slept throughout that day, and around 9:00 p.m., I lay down with him but did not go to sleep. I stayed up watching him as he slept.

Periodically, Larry would get up and go to the bathroom; the last time he did this, he began to stumble. I got up, helped him back to bed, and then went into the living room. I prayed, asking God for direction, because I knew something was very wrong, and I needed Him to direct me. By this time, it was about 12:30 a.m. I felt led to call Larry's sister, Diane, to let her know that I was going to take Larry to the local hospital. I realized I needed someone to help me get him into the car, because if he fell, I wouldn't be able to lift him, as he is five feet eleven and I am five feet three. Consequently, I called Cliff and Jeanette Hill, and thankfully, they responded. I knew that time was of the essence, and an ambulance would have taken too long to get to us.

As I waited for the Hills to arrive, I got Larry dressed and made sure we had the necessary credentials for checking into the hospital. After I had gotten everything together, our friends arrived, and Brother Hill and their son, Jaye, sat Larry in the chair with rollers that we kept in the bedroom. Then they rolled him into the kitchen and then into the garage, where they had parked their vehicle. We were on our way. However, nothing could have prepared me for what would happen when we got to the hospital.

VICTORIOUS, OVERCOMING FAITH

FAITH IS LIKE A DOOR OR A WINDOW IN the realm of the spirit. It gives God an opening to move and change things supernaturally. It hooks the spiritual realm and the natural realm together so God's will can be done for us here on earth just like it's done in heaven.

God has a will for our lives as children of God. He tells us so in His Word, in 3 John 2: "Beloved, I wish above all things that thou mayest prosper and be in health, even as thy soul prospereth." Three kinds of blessing are found in His will: (1) material prosperity, (2) bodily healing and health, and (3) soul salvation. In this chapter, I will be talking about the second kind of blessing, healing and health.

When we reached the hospital, the hospital personnel took us right into the triage station, where they made a quick assessment of Larry, and then they took us to a larger room in the ER. The ER doctor and several other attendants began to work on Larry. A CAT scan and X-ray of his chest were completed, as his breathing was very rapid. The doctor then called me into one of the empty rooms and said they had seen many lesions all over his chest walls. He further stated that because Larry's breathing was so rapid, they were afraid he would tire himself out, and his heart would become affected. Their plan was to induce a medical coma, put him on life support to assist with his breathing, and transport him to St Patrick's Hospital in Lake Charles.

At this point, I remember crying. His sister, Diane; my sister Brenda; our daughter-in-law, Lisa; and our sons, Omar and Ali were all there, so I asked the doctor to explain to them what he had just told me. He did, and then we were asked to go into the ER waiting room as they prepared Larry for the intubation. As we were waiting, one of the nurses came out and said that his heart had stopped, but they were trying to bring him back. I heard what she said, but for some reason, my mind would not allow me to comprehend it. It was as if my comprehension was momentarily suspended. I believe that the Lord, at that moment, shielded my mind so that I would not say anything against His will for Larry. He knew what He wanted to do, and any negative word spoken into the atmosphere could have thwarted His plan. So I remained supernaturally calm, and the nurse returned to the ER room. About ten minutes later, she came back out and said, "They got him back." I wouldn't know the depths of those ten minutes until we got to Lake Charles.

Some minutes later, they had completed the procedure, the ambulance had arrived, and we were on our way to St Patrick's. I rode in the ambulance with him, in front with the driver. When we arrived at the hospital, they carried Larry into the ICU unit, and I was told to wait in the ICU waiting room. When they finished getting him situated, then I would be able to see him. I was basically numb and tired from lack of sleep (at this time it was early afternoon). I remember crying and crying.

Soon my phone began to ring. It was from our church family: Brother Don Robinson and his wife, Tina, and also Brother Hector and his wife, Maria. They had gone to Beauregard Memorial Hospital after receiving the news of Larry's condition but of course were informed he was not there. I told them where we were, and they set off to come to us. In the meantime, my sister Brenda had informed our daughter-in-law Celestine of the news. Celestine happened to be in Lake Charles at Sam's Club, but upon hearing the news, she dropped everything and came to me. What a blessing she was! She remained with me from that Monday until Friday, making sure I remembered to take my medications, and that I ate in order to keep up my strength.

Perhaps an hour after Celestine arrived, our church family arrived. Only two persons at a time were allowed into ICU, so Brother Don and Brother Hector were able to see him. I was able to see him four times a day for one hour each visit. On that first day, Larry was immediately started on emergency dialysis. It seems the myeloma had shut down his kidneys. The nephrologist, Dr. Ahad Lodhi, ordered immediate dialysis because Larry had begun to swell. His fingers, arms, and legs had swollen to the point that it looked as if they would pop wide open if you stuck him with a pin. It was hard to look at him in that condition, but I knew God was right there with him.

When I visited him in the ICU unit each day, I talked to him, read the Word of God to him, and played gospel music because I knew it was important for his spirit man to stay strong. Fortunately, the spirit never sleeps, though our flesh gets tired and requires rest. It was Larry's spirit man that needed the most attention at this time to fight the spiritual battle being waged against him. Even though he was in an induced coma, I knew he could hear me.

My times with him were very important, and I did not waste one moment of them. We were in a fight for his very life, but I knew we would win. I had to believe that and not look at the body lying in the hospital bed. Rather, I had to focus on the One who was in control of that body. I didn't know how long I would have to fight, but God was preparing me for the many days ahead when I would have to function on only a few hours of rest at night, nights when I would play gospel music until I fell asleep.

During this time, a scripture came to mind: "Thou wilt keep him in perfect peace, whose mind is stayed on thee: because he trusteth in thee" (Isa. 26). This was exactly where I was living at the time. I had to keep my mind focused directly on the Lord—it was imperative. My husband's very life depended upon it. I was not going to let him down, and I certainly was not going to let my Lord and Savior down. The Lord had anointed me for this task, so I had no other recourse but to obey.

Dr. Lodhi talked with me on the evening of that first day in the hospital and said, "Your husband is a very sick man; if he makes it past twenty-four hours, we will know what to do next." Again, the Lord did not allow me to fully comprehend what he was saying. He shielded my understanding for that moment. The next day would be a very important day.

THE FIGHT WAS ON!

THE NEXT MORNING, MY HUSBAND WAS still alive. Praise the Lord! I went in to see him at 9:00 a.m., the first visitation time for the day. The dialysis machine was in the room, and the hospital staff explained that he would receive dialysis for three continual days, which was the emergency protocol for someone in his condition. The nurse in attendance said they would begin weaning him off the breathing tube. At this time, he was breathing on his own at approximately 20 percent capacity. She also explained that she was giving him simple commands to follow so they could determine how much of his brain power was still functioning. Larry had been lifeless for eight to ten minutes. According to the nurse, people out that long normally do not have much brain activity. However, Larry was responding very well to her commands. I told her it was only by the power of God that he was able to respond in that way. He had so many people praying for him, so many accessing the throne room of God on his behalf, that there was no way he was going to lie there without a response. I had kept in contact with Pastors George Lee and Karen Glass, updating them on Larry's condition. They in turn were communicating the information to the congregation.

On the third day of Larry's stay in ICU, the Lord prompted me to praise. I had already sent a text to the pastor to ask the congregation to praise at church service that night. When I went into ICU that morning, I knew what I needed to do. I had awakened that morning with a song by Darwin Hobbs and Detrick Haddon on my mind, "He's Able." I called my sister Marie and asked her to find it and text the link to me, which she did. I marched into the ICU room ready for battle.

As I entered, Larry was awake, so I told him I was going to play music. I put on the song, and as the music played, I began to praise God. I stood at the foot of Larry's bed, lifted my hands, and began to praise and cry out to the Lord. I did this until one of the nurses came and closed the door. I apologized that the music may have been too loud; after all, this was the ICU unit. She replied that it didn't bother her, and that she enjoyed it. I continued to praise until it was time for me to leave. For the remainder of that day, each time I went into his room, I brought music and praised God.

In an earlier chapter, I shared that I had to praise in order to make it through the radiation treatments I had to endure. Once again, I had to praise in this fight for my husband's life. Praise is a weapon! Second Chronicles 20 makes this very clear. In this chapter, we read that Jehoshaphat was faced with a grave situation. An enemy was closing in on him, and he could not see a way out. His first reaction was to fear, but that didn't last long, because verse 3 says he proclaimed a fast. As a result, the Lord's Spirit came upon Jahaziel and spoke through him, saying, "Thus saith the Lord unto you, Be not afraid nor dismayed by reason of this great multitude; for the battle is not yours, but God's" (v. 15). With this word of encouragement from the Lord, Jehoshaphat began to worship and praise the Lord. The next day, he appointed singers to go out before the army, praising God and the beauty of holiness. Jehoshaphat put his faith into action, believed the word of the Lord, and was not defeated.

In this same way, I put my faith into action, obeying what the Lord had told me to do—praise. I was trusting Him, knowing He was not a God who failed. He had never failed me yet, and I did not think for one minute that He would begin now. The following day, the nurse said they would remove the breathing tube on Friday, as Larry was now breathing at 80 percent on his own. I was ecstatic. God had moved in response to the praise sent up to His throne room. On Friday the tube was removed, and on Saturday we were moved out of ICU.

FAITH UNDER FIRE

IN THE NEW ROOM, LARRY WAS ALERT, but he did not talk very much, possibly because the breathing tube had made his throat very sore. He was not very strong because he had been lying in bed for so long, which saps your strength more and more the longer you lie in it. As a result, I took care of him just as I did my children when they were newly born. I didn't wait for the hospital staff to give him a bath. If they didn't come by a certain time, I called housekeeping for sheets, pillowcases, blankets, and towels, and I bathed him myself. The only help I needed was in making the bed. I couldn't maneuver that task alone with him lying in it, so I did ask for help with that. I didn't mind at all doing any of this for him. It was part of the marriage vows I had taken many years ago, "in sickness and in health."

Additionally, as I mentioned earlier, the Lord had already told me that He had anointed me for this time. There is absolutely no way I could have done it without His anointing. It would have been too hard. I was fighting a battle from the war room of spontaneous faith. I was doing as the Word of God says: "Fight the good fight of faith, lay hold on eternal life, whereunto thou art also called, and hast professed a good profession before many witnesses" (1 Tim. 6:12).

I have learned that in order to fight the good fight of faith, we have to lay hold of whatever we are asking and believing for, and we have to confess it is ours. We do not give up without a fight, but what do we use to fight? Our faith! Faith is a choice; it is a choice we make every day to believe that Jesus is who He says He is and that He can do what He says He can do. Proverbs 3:5 says it like this: "Trust in the Lord with all thine heart; and lean not unto thine own understanding" (emphasis added).

Faith (trust) and understanding are not the same thing. We trust God with our heart, not our head. The enemy will interject thoughts into our minds to try to make us believe that a fleeting thought is the same as wavering. Just because a feeling or thought crosses our mind, however, that doesn't mean we changed our decision to believe in our heart. This is why God tells us up front not to lean on our own understanding; that is, our own reasoning, thoughts, or feelings. If the enemy can get to us in the reasoning realm, he can defeat us.

I was faced with a situation in which I had no under-standing of what to do. On Sunday, I began to notice that Larry was not the same as when he first came out of ICU. At first, he had been able to sit on the side of the bed, propped up with pillows. But now, he was fatigued and sleeping throughout most of the day. He had a few visitors but was not able to communicate with them. I felt uneasy but held onto faith. I knew that God would work this out.

That night at shift change, I asked the nurse to check his blood sugar level, thinking perhaps it was elevated. She did as I requested, but the level was in a normal range. I lay down on the cot in the room and began to pray, asking God to give me His direction. I must have drifted off to sleep, because when I awakened, it was 3:00 a.m. Larry was sleeping but making those funny sounds again. God then directed me to get up and begin praying the prayers in a book that Donna, a sister in Christ, had compiled for me. I immediately did what He directed, and walked and prayed. At 5:00 a.m., the Lord led me to send a text to Pastor George Lee Glass, asking him to have whoever would do so to call my cell phone and leave a message of encouragement for Larry. I would play it so that he could hear it.

By now, it was time for a new shift change. I directed the new nurse's attention to my husband's changed behavior. I also noticed some yellow discharge coming out of the corner of his mouth. She immediately went to inform the doctor. The doctor came into the room and asked how long he had been like that, to which I replied that I had first noticed the change last night. He then ordered respiratory personnel to come in and take a look. The respiratory therapist indicated that Larry had begun to aspirate, and he was going to have to suction off the fluid that was beginning to fill his lungs. He pulled off as much fluid as he could and then notified the doctor. The doctor came back into the room and immediately ordered Larry back to ICU, which meant that I had move all our belongings back to the ICU waiting room, where I would remain while he was in ICU.

God, of course, knew ahead of time all that was going to happen, and He had placed it upon the hearts of two sisters in Christ, Reneé and Robbie, to come visit me. They were thus able to help me get all our things moved down to the ICU area. Praise the Lord! Not only did these two women come to visit, but they also brought more items to me. God was certainly taking care of little old me in such a magnificent way.

The enemy, however, had other plans, as he began to interject thoughts into my mind, telling me, Now look at this. You were doing all that prayer and praising and worshiping God, and now look, your husband is back in ICU again. I promptly ordered him to get out of my mind. I cast down those thoughts and directed every thought to be subjected to Jesus Christ. I told the devil that he was a liar and God was the truth, that this was only a setback and God was still in control. I did not understand why this was happening, but I was not going to let go of my stance of faith.

We had many visitors that night. Elder Gregory MacFadden came to see Larry and was able to go into the ICU room. Larry began to smile as Elder Greg spoke to him and prayed over him. We had church in that ICU room! When we returned to the ICU waiting area, a large group of people was there: Minister Rita Harris; Karen Williams; my sister Brenda Olivier; Brother Bubba and his wife, Tina White; Sister Linda Young, and Brother Larry Taylor. (This last man has the same name as my husband and belongs to the same body of believers that we do. My husband likes to tease him and say that he is Larry number one.) God sent all these sisters and brothers in Christ to provide me with the encouragement I needed at that time. We stood in a circle, and as these precious believers prayed and worshiped the Lord, a surge of renewed strength took hold of me. Other people were also in the ICU waiting room, and many of them joined with us in prayer. What a time! I was so humbled that God thought enough of me to send this body of believers to give me a boost of spiritual energy. I had sweet sleep that night in the ICU waiting room.

The following morning was Larry's birthday and our thirtieth anniversary. I went to the gift shop to buy a birthday and an anniversary card, still on the spiritual high from the night before. When I entered his room in ICU, he was awake. I read his cards to him, and we watched TBN on television together. After my visit, I returned to the ICU waiting room. The doctor arrived shortly afterward and said he was going to release Larry to return to his regular room in the evening. I asked him to send us to a different floor this time, and the doctor agreed, sending us to the fifth floor. So once more, I had to get our things ready to move.

A very nice older gentleman, Mr. Wiley, was the attendant in ICU during the daytime hours. He watched out for all of us during our stay. If we needed extra blankets or towels, he took care of that. At night, a young lady named Lisa Cross took his place and checked on us. I was very appreciative to both of them for their compassionate spirits in seeing to our needs. Mr. Wiley, the day attendant, helped me move all our things into the room on the fifth floor. He also brought me a cot to sleep on, as I had been sleeping in a chair in the ICU waiting room. It felt so good to stretch out on that cot that night. Larry did not have to be readmitted to ICU during the rest of his stay there in St. Patrick's Hospital.

WITNESSING GOD'S PLAN OF FREEDOM

GOD ALWAYS HAS A PLAN OF FREEDOM. When His people cried out to Him in Egypt, He put His plan into action. The blood on the doorposts opened the way to liberty and a new identity for His people. Of course, Jesus was the ultimate Passover Lamb. He lived, died, and rose again to bring us liberty from the bondage of death, hell, and the grave—that is, freedom from control, interference, obligation, restriction, and the rule of Satan.

This is what He did for my husband. During his tenure at St. Patrick's, I had no idea of the actions taking place behind the scenes, nor the depths of what would be required to move us to the next phase in Larry's recovery.

The word recovery means the following:

> To recuperate or regain what has been lost or taken
> To regain health or get well
> To return to a state of control or authority
> To regain or reclaim land or substances from waste
> To retrieve a person from a bad state
> To reclaim, demand, or decree that restoration will begin

Larry had gone as far as he could go at St. Patrick's Hospital, and it was now time to go a step further in the recovery process.

The Holy Spirit began to speak to Dr. Mahesh Pandya, Larry's primary care doctor in DeRidder, and he took action on the words he was hearing. Dr. Pandya had not forgotten about us while we were in Lake Charles; he called frequently to check on the status of my husband. During our last conversation, I'm sure he heard the concern in my voice, and I believe the Spirit of God began to advise him on what we needed to do in order to save my husband's life.

God had not brought Larry back from death for him to die again. God does not do anything haphazardly or halfway. Everything He does is perfect and well executed. So the plan of God began unfold through the obedience of Dr. Pandya. What the enemy had meant for evil, God was turning around for Larry's good.

One of the doctors on the team at St. Patrick's explained to me that he had been talking with a doctor in DeRidder named Dr. Pandya. He asked me if I had talked to him, and I answered, "Yes, Dr. Pandya has called quite frequently to check on Larry; he has been very concerned with his status." The doctor further stated that Dr. Pandya had spoken with Dr. Krina Patel at M. D. Anderson in Houston, Texas, the same doctor we had seen during our weeklong stay when a treatment plan was being established for Larry. After speaking with Dr. Pandya, Dr. Patel had agreed to treat Larry for the multiple myeloma.

The doctor explained that the myeloma was the root cause of Larry's condition, and unless it was treated, he would not regain his health. He went on to say that the hospital team was making arrangements for Larry to be transported to Houston, and I could ride with him. I was ecstatic. A couple of days later, we were informed that we would soon be leaving Lake Charles and heading to Houston.

Two days later, the ambulance arrived around 10:00 p.m. to pick us up. We were both so excited. We didn't know what we were facing, but we knew we were facing it together and with God's guidance. I sat in the front with one of the ambulance personnel, and the other attendant was stationed in the back with Larry. I prayed the entire trip because Larry had to sit on a gurney in an almost upright position. My concern was for the pressure wound that he had developed during his inactivity in the hospital. I knew it could be rough sitting in that position for the length of time it would take to get to Houston. But thanks be to God! When we reached our destination around 3:30 a.m., Larry was in good spirits and had actually conversed with the ambulance attendant during the ride.

We were taken to the ER department in order to get checked in, even though the hospital staff was awaiting our arrival. At one point during the intake process, the nurse asked if Larry could stand and get on the scales to determine his weight. Now Larry had not been out of bed since his arrival at St Patrick's, so I was not sure if he would have the strength to comply with this request. To my surprise, with assistance from the ambulance personnel, he was able to stand on the scales. It brought tears to my eyes to see him standing there.

After completing the intake, we were taken to an area in the ER to await Dr. Krina Patel's assistant, who would be meeting with us. As we waited, many people were coming in and out, asking us questions and gathering information.

Larry greeted everyone with a smile and cheerful banter. Dr. Patel's assistant soon arrived and advised us of the plan for the day. The team would immediately start Larry on his first round of chemo. I was amazed at how quickly things were moving, but relieved that we were finally beginning the eradication of the myeloma cells invading his body.

At one point, a wound care supervisor entered the room, asking to see the pressure wound. As she inspected it, she asked me if I had seen it, to which I replied, "No." She asked me to come over and look at it. When I saw the large wound on his backside, I wondered how in the world he had endured the long ride from Louisiana to Texas without complaint. I thanked God for His faithfulness, mercy, and grace in bringing my husband across the state line without discomfort. The supervisor immediately began to take care of the wound and placed into his medical records the protocol to be followed from this day forward.

The hospital staff had taken the liberty of ordering lunch for us. As we waited for the room to be made ready for our stay, I fed my husband lunch. He had not eaten very well in Lake Charles, but seemed to enjoy the meal being served to him. After we finished eating, the room was ready, and hospital transportation assisted us in getting there.

I could not believe my eyes when I saw the room. It was spacious, clean, and had a beautiful view of the medical center. Larry's side of the room was the side next to the door, while my side was next to the window and featured my own private television. In another part of the room was the bath with a walk-in shower. I thanked God for His faithfulness again, as I realized I would be able to rest in comfort and also enjoy a long, hot shower. True to their word, the nurses began to prepare the IV's for Larry's first round of chemo. It would take several hours for the medicine to complete its cycle. Thus began the days of our lives at M. D. Anderson.

In 1 Peter 5:6–7, the Word of God speaks of the growing up process as we continually present ourselves to God in prayer: "Therefore humble yourselves under the mighty hand of God, that He may exalt you in due time, casting all your care upon Him, for He cares for you" (emphasis added). When is "due time"? It is when we are mature enough for God to promote us to our next phase of responsibility and leadership authority without our childishness derailing the blessing. My husband and I were in another phase of the growing up process.

As I watched Larry go through each step of the required treatment, I marveled that he never complained. A continual stream of doctors, nurses, and other attendants came in and out of the room, even at night. The ones who came around 3:00 a.m., he called his ninjas. He always had something humorous to say to them, which would make them laugh. I also marveled that he did not experience nausea or an upset stomach from the extensive amounts of chemo he was receiving. I knew that God was not allowing the meds to adversely affect him, and I continually thanked God for the goodness and mercy He was extending to my husband.

Each passing day brought new ways of doing things. God was breaking off our old mindsets and bringing us both into avenues of freedom. His Spirit was setting us free from old bondages that had previously held us in a vise grip of fear. He was letting us know that as we submitted to Him and this newfound freedom in Him,

He would surround us with His righteousness, and our healing would break forth speedily. For you see, it is not the letter of the law that brings us freedom, but His Spirit that makes us free.

He was helping us see that He is the Great Physician. Even though we were surrounded by physicians at the top of their fields, it was in Christ that we were to put our total trust for healing. We certainly did not want to take anything away from the doctors and nurses at M. D. Anderson—we thanked the Lord continually for them—but at the top in center field was our Lord and Savior Jesus Christ. It was to Him that we gave, and will continue to give, our utmost allegiance. To God be the glory for all the things that He did for us during that time and that He continues to do daily for us.

We had to learn to trust Him in spite of what our eyes might see, so it was learning to trust Him by faith and not by sight. What we saw physically was only a temporary thing, but our faith would bring the manifestation of deliverance and healing. We were like little children who had learned to walk and were now running with carefree abandon, knowing that our Father had already gone before us, clearing the path. We didn't have to worry about anything tripping us up or making us stumble and fall. God had already prepared the way. That is what He does—He makes a way when there seems to be no way. We saw this with our very own eyes.

As we took one day at a time, the Lord brought healing and health to Larry's bones. He became strong again. Each day a physical therapist worked on his walking ability. He had been bedridden so long that he had to learn to walk again. The therapist had to teach him how to get out of bed and use a walker to bring himself to a standing position. Then they would walk down the hall together. In the first few days, the therapist would secure a safety belt around him and hold it as they walked. But gradually, as Larry learned to walk steadily without it, the therapist did not need to use it.

There were also occupational therapists that taught him how to take care of his daily personal needs, such as shaving, showering, etc. It is amazing how we take these little things for granted, until one day when we are not able to do them. What a humbling experience this was for him! Larry had always been an independent, strong man, and now someone had to show him how to do the most basic, personal things he had always done for himself. However, he took it all in stride, completing the tasks required of him without complaint.

Larry continued to make great progress, and we finally could see the light at the end of the tunnel. We had spent a total of twenty-one days in M. D. Anderson, and it was now time for his discharge. Larry had asked his friend Mr. Earl to pick us up, to which he graciously agreed. So we bade farewell to the staff who had taken such great care of us and headed home to Louisiana.

RESTORED AND REVIVED

WE ARRIVED HOME AROUND MIDNIGHT
and needed to get to sleep quickly because the very
next day we had to go to the DaVita Dialysis Center.
Larry would need to go to the center three times a week,
but that was not the only appointment he had to keep.
The next week, we had to return to Houston to see his
oncologist, Dr. Krina Patel, for follow-up. At that visit, Dr.
Patel said the lab work showed that the cancer cells had
decreased from over five thousand to only three hundred.
She was ecstatic about this decrease, and so were we.
We knew it was the work of the Lord, that His hand was
visible in the lab report.

We were advised to follow through with the next part of
the treatment, which was to be on steroids along with
receiving chemo injections; and then later, the final part
of the treatment would be a stem cell transplant. Dr. Patel
stated that she would allow Dr. Mahesh Pandya, Larry's
primary care physician, to administer the shots, thereby
relieving us of having to travel to Houston every week for
the injections. We were so relieved to hear that because
the traffic in that city is quite heavy; I certainly did not want

to have to drive there every week. I thanked God for His kindness and favor.

The following month was very hectic, to say the least. Nonetheless, every morning Larry would awaken with a smile and say, "Okay, what is on the agenda for today?" Then, in the next breath, he would proclaim, "Don't stop, don't quit!" Even though I was very tired, I would take a deep breath and push myself forward into the day's plan. I thought that if my husband, who had undergone the most trying time of his life, could get up with a smile every morning, then I certainly could keep pressing forward.

I would think about God's Word in Isaiah 40:28–31:

> Hast thou not known? Hast thou not heard, that the Everlasting God, the Lord, the Creator of the ends of the earth, fainteth not, neither is weary? There is no searching of His understanding. He giveth power to the faint; and to them that have no might He increaseth strength. Even the youths shall faint and be weary, and the young men shall utterly fall: But they that wait upon the Lord shall renew their strength; they shall mount up with wings as eagles; they shall run, and not be weary; and they shall walk and not faint.

My husband, who had died at the beginning of this new year and was restored and revived by God Almighty, understood that when you wait upon God, when you keep pressing forward, God will meet you right where you are. Then you understand that you are not doing this in your own strength, but in the strength of almighty God. This is the God whose greatness is declared many times in Scripture, but I will declare only one of them:

Bless the Lord, O my soul. O Lord my God, thou art very great; thou art clothed with honour and majesty. Who coverest thyself with light as with a garment: who stretchest out the heavens like a curtain: Who layeth the beams of His chambers in the waters: who maketh the clouds His chariot: who walketh upon the wings of the wind: Who maketh His angels spirits; His ministers a flaming fire: Who laid the foundations of the earth, that it should not be removed forever. Thou coveredst it with the deep as with a garment: the waters stood above the mountains.
Psalm 104:1–6

My husband understood experientially what it meant to wait upon the Lord because during those eight to ten minutes when his heart had stopped, he had no strength, no power, and no might. But God!

I began to follow my husband's lead, and every morning, I would look forward to whatever the day would hold because I knew that each day was precious. Today is all we have because tomorrow is not promised. We both had learned a powerful lesson about life that we would never forget.

We continued to keep appointments and travel often from Louisiana to Texas. Finally, the time came to make preparations for the stem cell transplant. We had been given all the information about the procedure during an orientation class at M. D. Anderson. Also, a social worker was assisting me with making plans to stay in Houston while Larry recuperated from the transplant.

During a conversation with the social worker one day, I was told that his insurance would not be accepted for the transplant. I was stunned. We had not anticipated this turn of events, and for a few days, I didn't know what to do. I then called my friend Reneé Abshire and she prayed this prayer:

> Lord, we ask You right now for Your direction in this situation. We don't understand all the things that are happening. But one thing we do know is that You order our steps. You make a way for us when there seems to be no way. We ask for Your favor, and we ask for Your guidance. We thank You, Lord, that You have been healing Larry, and You know exactly what his body needs. If You shut the door for this procedure, we know that You are healing him completely without it. I ask for Your peace and Your strength over Larry and Kathy right now and in the coming days to know that You have ordered everything from this point, and You will complete what You have begun in Larry's life. In Jesus' name, amen.

After the prayer, I felt strengthened, so I called the insurance company again. I spoke with a representative who suggested that I call Houston Methodist to see if they would accept our insurance for the transplant. I did just that and was told that they would accept his insurance, and because he had met all his deductibles for the year, there would be nothing out of pocket for us to pay. Consequently, we never received a bill pertaining to the stem cell transplant, which cost over $100,000 according to the statements we received. What a mighty God we serve! I had tried to arrange circumstances so that Larry could continue his treatments at M. D. Anderson, but God shut the door because He knew that the next phase was to take place at Houston Methodist. So no matter how hard I tried, I could not get the door at M. D. Anderson to open.

The pre-transplant testing began on July 22, 2018, at Houston Methodist. We would be there until July 24, as Larry underwent heart stress testing, pulmonary function testing, a PET scan, blood work, a psychosocial visit, and a bone marrow biopsy. We actually stayed over another night because I did not know how Larry would feel after the bone marrow biopsy. I didn't want him to have to travel hundreds of miles in discomfort. We thus returned home on July 25.

On Thursday, September 6, 2018, we returned to Houston Methodist for stem cell collection. We went to the hospital the following day, Friday, to begin a series of shots to increase his stem cells. I was shown how to administer the injections because that particular wing of the hospital was not open on the weekends, so I would need to do them myself. I was very nervous, to say the least. But my trust was in God, and He brought us both through.

On Monday, September 10, 2018, Larry was admitted into the hospital, and the stem cell collection was started. For three days, they collected his good cells and stored them in a freezer until it was time to place them back into his bone marrow. The hospital personnel collected enough for two transplants, if needed. Their hope was that he would need only one transplant, and that was our prayer as well, because I did not want him to have to go through another transplant procedure.

We returned home the following day to await a call from the transplant team. We received the call on September 25 and was informed that one of the bags had been contaminated as the result of an infection from Larry's dialysis catheter. Therefore, they would have only one bag at their disposal. We were not concerned about that, though. We had asked the Lord for only one time to go through the process, so one bag was all we needed. His doctor advised us to return on October 14, 2018, for the transplant.

We returned to Houston a day early, with a dear couple, Elders Greg and Denise MacFadden, providing the transportation. We checked into the Marriott Hotel that night in order to be close to the hospital, but I did not realize just how close we were until later that evening. I became thirsty and told Larry I was going to find us some bottled water. I figured I could go to the snack dispensers. I walked to the elevators and got off on the third floor. As I turned to the left, I noticed that things began to look familiar. As I kept walking, I saw a sign that read "Houston Methodist Elevators." I gasped as I realized that the hotel was connected to the hospital. All we would have to do in the morning would be to check out of the hotel and take the elevator down, and we would be right where we needed to be to check into the hospital.

Larry was admitted into the hospital the next day, and I was with him during the entire stay. The doctor had advised us that prior to receiving the stem cells, Larry would be given a very strong dose of chemo to kill any cancer cells that might still be alive in his body. Unfortunately, this would cause his hair to fall out and could also cause stomach infections or mouth ulcers. We had to follow a very strict protocol, with washing hands of the utmost importance.

They soon brought the chemo and administered it intravenously. They also brought popsicles for Larry to eat for thirty minutes; this would help with the mouth sores. My sister Marie sent two prayers that I prayed while this process was going on:

Heavenly Father, we pray that You take out all the impurities from all the medications Larry and everybody else are taking today. Heavenly Father, do not let any of the side effects harm Larry's body or the bodies of others from the medications they may be taking. Amen.

Dear Lord, touch the sheep of Your flock who are in medical need right now. In Jesus' name, amen.

On October 17, 2018, Larry's stem cells were returned to his body It took only fifteen minutes for the process, while the extraction of the cells had taken two days. Amazing!

STRENGTH TO ENDURE

THE DOCTORS AT HOUSTON METHODIST
wanted us to remain in the hospital for at least two weeks
after the transplant to see how his body was reacting, and
then for another two more weeks in the Houston area.
While we were in the hospital, Larry developed a stomach
infection. This was a common occurrence, according to
the doctors, but I was still in war mode. On October 24,
2018, I began the day with this prayer:

Let the weak say, "I am strong!" God, we thank You for a
strong immune system. Larry's body is healed, and that
means it is equipped with everything needed for a healthy
life. We thank You for Your promise of long life and life
more abundantly. I rebuke this issue of stomach infection,
and I rebuke the source of it—now. In Jesus' name, I pray.
Thank You, Lord. Amen.

My word for that day was "strength to endure," and this
was my declaration:

Every plague, every sickness, every infection that
comes near Larry or me is stopped right now in

the mighty name of Jesus through the atonement of Jesus Christ.

Because of the infection, Larry could no longer go outside his room and walk the halls as he had in the beginning. However, exercise was very important to increase the blood cells necessary for his immune health. I thus continued to stand on God's Word and the prayer that I had prayed on October 24. I knew God was faithful and would not allow Larry's progress to be hindered, despite the lack of exercise. We continued to praise the Lord in the room and be encouraged by those who called and visited.

One day Larry received a big surprise when some of the men of Grace who had attended a retreat close to the Houston area stopped by to see him. It was Brothers Hill, White, Rivera, and David. Larry was so excited to have his brothers in Christ visit. What an encouragement it was to his soul! Larry had suffered an adverse reaction to the medication given to treat the stomach infection, so he had not felt like himself the night before. Consequently, the visit not only encouraged him, but the fellowship took his mind off the reaction of his body to the medication.

Praise the Lord! God is so faithful. He knows exactly what we need and when we need it. He placed Larry on the minds of these brothers in Christ, and they acted in obedience. I marveled as I looked at the black, white, and Hispanic men standing in a circle praying for my husband. What a glorious sight! It brought to my mind the scripture from Joel 2:29: "And also on My menservants and on My maidservants I will pour out My Spirit in those days." God's Spirit was being poured out in that room as men of different races poured out their souls to God. Men lifted their voices to God in the unity of the Spirit. Men prayed together for the healing of their brother in Christ.

We stayed at Houston Methodist until the first week of November 2018, and then we were released to an apartment we had rented. It was the cutest apartment; everything was in its place, so all we needed to do was to bring ourselves and our clothing. It was our home away from home. Both Larry and I enjoyed it because he could rest in the bedroom, and I could hang out in the living room so as not to disturb him. From both the bedroom and the living room, the apartment had a wonderful view of the swimming pool. When Larry was not sleeping, he could look out on it. Since it was fall, practically no one was in the pool, as very few would dare to venture out into that cold water.

Larry still had to take dialysis, but not at the hospital. I therefore set up treatments at Fresenius, and we used a Lyft for transportation. Also, Larry had been suffering with itching episodes, so when we went back to the hospital for his checkup, I told the doctor about it. The nurse practitioner, Audrey, asked if he had been given any new meds recently, and I informed her that his only new med was vancomycin. It was discontinued that very day, and from that day forward, the itching episodes lessened. His appetite also began to return, and he began to rest through the night.

The time soon came for us to go home. On November 16, 2018, we were released from Houston Methodist. We had gone to the hospital that morning, and all his blood work was good. Since the discontinuation of the vancomycin, he no longer suffered with the itching episodes. We thus returned to the apartment to await our son Ali, who was coming to pick us up. I had been packing and cleaning the day before in preparation of our departure. Our son soon arrived, and we made the long trek home from Texas to

Louisiana. We were so thankful for the journey, but so glad it was now over.

As Larry's blood count continued to increase, his risk for infection decreased. We still had to return to Houston Methodist for follow-up appointments, but there were no setbacks to the stem cell transplant. I believe in my heart that the Lord anointed my husband and me for this particular time and purpose. It is the power of God that gives us the ability to perform the purpose that He has given us. We all have a divine purpose, and no one can fulfill another person's purpose.

If you don't yet know your purpose, or if you don't think you have a purpose, search for God and allow Him to reveal it to you. Don't continue to wander aimlessly through life. Paul told Timothy, his spiritual son in the Lord, "Do not neglect the gift that is in you, which was given to you by prophecy with the laying on of the hands of the elder-ship" (1 Tim. 4:14). And again, in 2 Timothy 1:6, he said, "Therefore I remind you to stir up the gift of God which is in you through the laying on of my hands" (emphasis added). We need to stir up what may be lying dormant within us, the thing that only we as an individual can accomplish in this earth. To stir means to awake, to rise, reenkindle, to fan a flame. If you feel as though your flame has burned out, turn to the one who put the flame there in the beginning. Turn to Him in repentance, and He will forgive you and fan your flame afresh.

THE CONCLUSION OF THE MATTER

AS I COME TO THE END OF THIS MANU-
script, I must confess that it took two years for me to
complete the task of writing it. This is the year 2020, and
I began the book in the latter part of 2018. When I began
to write, I didn't realize how hard it would be as I remembered the events that happened to my husband and me
on this journey. Sometimes I had to step away from the
writing for a while, because each time I began, a fresh
wave of sorrow would come to my spirit, and tears would
begin to flow. But I pressed on as I was able and wrote
this conclusion in the beginning of July 2020. The following expresses my thoughts and feelings at the time.

As I write this conclusion, these three thoughts come
to my mind:

> I feel compelled.
> I feel an unction from the Holy Ghost.
> I feel the Spirit of compassion.

These three thoughts bring to mind the number nine. In a spiritual sense, this number represents a full cycle, finality, and divine completeness. With a great sense of urgency, I know the Holy Ghost is requesting that I get with it. Enough time has gone by. The Spirit of God is compelling me to go forward, to complete this cycle, to finalize the work that I began.

I feel the Spirit of compassion. It was said of our Lord and Savior in Matthew 9:36, "But when He saw the multitudes, He was moved with compassion for them, because they were weary and scattered, like sheep having no shepherd." I know there are those who are waiting for the words of this book to encourage them to hold on, not give up, and not give in.

I also know that timing is everything with God. Even though I intended for this book to be completed long before now, I am reminded of His words in Ecclesiastes 3:1, 17:

> "To everything there is a season, a time for every purpose under heaven.... I said in my heart, God shall judge the righteous and the wicked, for there is a time for every purpose and for every work" (emphasis added). Also, in Ecclesiastes 8:6, we read, "Because for every matter there is a time and judgment, though the misery of man increases greatly" (emphasis added).

I believe this time is very relevant for the ending of this book, especially in light of all the occurrences in the earth today. People are looking with fear at the ravages of the COVID-19 virus, while others do not even believe it is a reality. One thing, however, is absolutely sure, and that is that Jesus is returning to earth to gather His bride, those who have believed in His name and are the children of

God, as it says in John 1:12–13: "But as many as received Him, to them He gave the right to become children of God, to those who believe in His name: who were born, not of blood, nor of the will of the flesh, nor of the will of man, but of God."

Thank God for His forgiveness of sin, His cleansing power, and His making us alive to God. In other words, we have been regenerated, or spiritually reborn. Second Corinthians 5:17 explains it this way: "Therefore, if anyone is in Christ, he is a new creation; old things have passed away; behold, all things have become new." This is the spiritual rebirth. But it doesn't stop there; we also have a responsibility that comes with this rebirth. The Bible tells us that in verses 18–19: "Now all things are of God, who has reconciled us to Himself through Jesus Christ, and has given us the ministry of reconciliation, that is, that God was in Christ reconciling the world to Himself, not imputing their trespasses to them, and has committed to us the word of reconciliation" (emphasis added).

As I complete this task, I would like to leave with you what has been my mainstay for so many years—His Word. Nothing in this life is greater than the Word of God. I love His Word. The first thing I do each morning—or at least I try my best to do so—is to read His Word. I don't know what each day holds for me, but He does, so when I read His Word, I receive my direction. Even though things may get a little chaotic in that day, because I have put Him and His Word first, I find comfort, knowing that I am not alone and He is right there with me.

I recommend to you Jesus—the only One who can bring you through the terrible times you will face. He will not ever fail you. If you have drifted from Him, turn back at this very moment as you read these words of life. Allow them to go deep into the recesses of your heart and draw you back to the one who gave His life so that you might live an abundant life in this present world.

Be blessed by these words of life from the Holy Bible:

Truly my soul silently waits for God; from Him comes my salvation. He only is my rock and my salvation; He is my defense; I shall not be greatly moved. How long will you attack a man? You shall be slain, all of you, like a leaning wall and a tottering fence. They only consult to cast him down from his high position; they delight in lies; they bless with their mouth, but they curse inwardly. Selah. My soul, wait silently for God alone, for my expectation is from Him. He only is my rock and my salvation; He is my defense; I shall not be moved. In God is my salvation and my glory; the rock of my strength, and my refuge, is in God. Trust in Him at all times, you people; pour out your heart before Him; God is a refuge for us. Selah. Surely men of low degree are a vapor, men of high degree are a lie; if they are weighed on the scales, they are altogether lighter than vapor. Do not trust in oppression, nor vainly hope in robbery; if riches increase, do not set your heart on them. God has spoken once, twice I have heard this; that power belongs to God. Also to You, O Lord, belongs mercy; for You render to each one according to his work.
Psalm 62:1–12 NKJV

Blessed is the man whose strength is in You, whose heart is set on pilgrimage.... For a day in Your courts is better than a thousand. I would rather be a doorkeeper in the house of my God than dwell in the tents of wickedness. For the Lord God is a sun

and shield; the Lord will give grace and glory; no good thing will He withhold from those who walk uprightly. O Lord of hosts, blessed is the man who trusts in You!
Psalm 84:5, 10–12 NKJV

But those who wait on the Lord shall renew their strength; they shall mount up with wings like eagles, they shall run and not be weary, they shall walk and not faint.
Isaiah 40:31 NKJV

I will go in the strength of the Lord God; I will make mention of Your righteousness, of Yours only.
Psalm 71:16 NKJV

My flesh and my heart fail; but God is the strength of my heart and my portion forever.
Psalm 73:26 NKJV

ABOUT THE AUTHOR

KATHY ANN TAYLOR IS first and foremost a woman who loves the Lord and His people. Her passion for those who have been misused and abused was the driving force for this book.

She is the wife of Larry J. Taylor, and the Mother of three Sons. They reside in a small town of DeRidder, in the state of Louisiana, where their home is used as a ministry to those who have been wounded by the pressures of life. She has been blessed to be an intercessory prayer warrior; using this gift to pray for and on behalf of those to whom God directs.

CPSIA information can be obtained
at www.ICGtesting.com
Printed in the USA
BVHW071125230421
605721BV00004B/556